PRAISE FOR
WHAT THE FIRE IGNITED

"Shay's story of perseverance and sheer will is one that needs to be told and retold! His journey is both harrowing and hope filled."

—R.A. DICKEY
NL Cy Young Winner
Olympic Bronze Medalist

"This is an incredible story. Shay shares his amazing journey of overcoming countless obstacles and challenges to become a world-class athlete against insurmountable odds. It is a story of resilience, strength, family, and turning everything thrown at you into an opportunity. Read this and prepare to be inspired!"

—CRAIG ALEXANDER
Five-time Triathlon World Champion

"Utterly inspirational. Shay has constantly defied the odds, and his powerful, heart-wrenching, and ultimately uplifting story is a testament to the indomitable power of the human body and mind. It's a must read."

—CHRISSIE WELLINGTON
Four-time IRONMAN World Champion

"To call Shay Eskew superhuman is an understatement. Shay somehow turned an unthinkable tragedy into boundless inspiration. He bares his soul in What the Fire Ignited *and his story had me laughing, crying, but mostly cheering for this improbable hero. Go Shay!"*

—DEAN KARNAZES
TIME, "Top 100 Most Influential People in the World"
New York Times Bestselling Author

"A book that needed to be written now needs to read."

—JACK DALY

Three-time Amazon Bestselling Author

Fifteen-time IRONMAN

"What the Fire Ignited is a quick, fascinating read. Based on a personal tale of tragedy, it's an inspirational and gut-wrenching account of one man's determination which ultimately proves self-made success is possible despite tragedy and formidable obstacles. Told with self-deprecating humor, a lot of heart, and wistful charm, this compelling story forces you to empathize, do a little self-reflection, and ultimately walk away thinking, 'Man, I want to get to know this guy!'"

—CHANDA BELL

Author, *The Elf on the Shelf*, Writer and Director

"We can let the things that happen in our lives steer our trajectory in a way that is cumbersome and negative, or in a way that is triumphant, stronger, and more epic. Shay has chosen the latter. With the use of humor, family, community, and an amazing attitude, he has let the apparent 'obstacles' be the way to success."

—THAD BEATY

Sugarland Guitarist

Billboard Hit Songwriter and Producer

Multiple IRONMAN and Leadville Finisher

"Shay embodies the perseverance, strength, and tenacity we see throughout the entire IRONMAN community. He proves that 'Anything Is Possible.'"

—ANDREW MESSICK

President and CEO, IRONMAN

WHAT THE
FIRE
IGNITED

HOW **LIFE'S WORST**
HELPED ME ACHIEVE **MY BEST**

WHAT THE

FIRE

IGNITED

SHAY ESKEW

Advantage®

Published by Advantage, Charleston, South Carolina.
Member of Advantage Media Group.

ADVANTAGE is a registered trademark, and the Advantage colophon is a trademark of Advantage Media Group, Inc.

Printed in the United States of America.

10 9 8 7 6 5 4 3 2 1

ISBN: 978-1-64225-027-5
LCCN: 2018955778

Cover and layout design by Melanie Cloth.

This publication is designed to provide accurate and authoritative information in regard to the subject matter covered. It is sold with the understanding that the publisher is not engaged in rendering legal, accounting, or other professional services. If legal advice or other expert assistance is required, the services of a competent professional person should be sought.

Advantage Media Group is proud to be a part of the Tree Neutral® program. Tree Neutral offsets the number of trees consumed in the production and printing of this book by taking proactive steps such as planting trees in direct proportion to the number of trees used to print books. To learn more about Tree Neutral, please visit **www.treeneutral.com**.

Advantage Media Group is a publisher of business, self-improvement, and professional development books and online learning. We help entrepreneurs, business leaders, and professionals share their Stories, Passion, and Knowledge to help others Learn & Grow. Do you have a manuscript or book idea that you would like us to consider for publishing? Please visit **advantagefamily.com** or call **1.866.775.1696**.

To Brooke, for your unconditional love, unwavering trust I will always do what is right for our family and selfless dedication to being the best mother for our kids. To my kids, Olivia, Maddox, Asher, Beckett and Stella for giving me renewed purpose in life and reminding me two ordinary people bound by love can create something extraordinary. To my parents, for always encouraging me to pursue my dreams and telling me I could do anything if I put my mind to it.

TABLE OF CONTENTS

===
. . . . .

FOREWORD

I'm a 69-year-old man with a life of significant achievement. I don't say this from a point of ego, but rather one of deep experience. It's not often that I run into people that truly impress me with their accomplishments, let alone coming from a base or foundation of serious life challenges. It's in this vein that I write this forward for Shay Eskew, as he is one impressive individual!

If you are looking to be inspired, look no further than *What the Fire Ignited*. If you are looking for lessons learned in overcoming adversity, look no further than the pages of this book. If you are looking for the route to turn negatives into positives, you have found it.

How do you explain Shay Eskew, having 65 percent of his body burned at eight years old and going on, by his mid-forties and some 35 surgeries later, to completing four full IRONMANs and 25 IRONMAN 70.3 races, happily married with five kids, and in the top 1 percent of his field in business? Throughout this book, you will learn many lessons to such success. Sure, Shay will underscore his early commitment to his vision and goals. He will, rightfully so, demonstrate the power of proven systems and processes. The taking of measured risks, the power of a sense of humor, and the leverage of networking and relationships all clearly come through in his journey. You will learn so much as you join Shay in his retrospective view of his life to date.

But, as Shay demonstrates throughout his life journey, the simple answer is grit. As Shay latched on to early in life, the great determinant in the direction our life takes is our commitment to stay focused on our vision and goals, and to have the grit to keep plugging (day by day) despite any obstacles thrown our way. Personally, I call it "How bad do you want it?" You will find that Shay wanted success in sport, family, business, and life. Once you have finished reading his story, I suggest you reach out to say thanks for his sharing and connect with this remarkable man.

I know from personal experience that my life trajectory has been enhanced as a result of our meeting. Guaranteed he will light a fire within you as well.

With respect,

Jack Daly

(Note: Shay here. Jack didn't go into his background, but I suggest visiting www.jackdaly.net to see this dynamo. Having built six companies in the USA into national platforms, authored three number one Amazon Bestsellers, completed marathons on all seven continents and in all 50 states, completed 15 IRONMANs, and became a top-rated speaker in the field of sales and sales management, Jack truly speaks from experience. I humbly thank him for his generous words above.)

INTRODUCTION
Forged by Fire

At age eight, my life was altered forever. I was set afire by a neighbor's teenage daughter and, after enduring over 35 surgeries, over 65 percent of my body was left covered in scars. Who would have thought an eight-year-old, told by doctors he'd never be competitive in sports again, would one day compete in 10 triathlon world championships across four continents, including the IRONMAN World Championships in Kona?

My life has not been one of usual comforts, but it has been an extraordinary one. It's a life I'm grateful for and, given the opportunity, I wouldn't change a thing. From my journey to hell and back, to crossing the finish line in the lava fields of Kona, to marrying the girl of my dreams and having five amazing kids 12 and under, to an amazing career, I've truly experienced extreme highs and lows. As we say in IRONMAN, anything is possible and embrace the suck!

As a result of the fire, my right arm was restricted to a 45-degree angle and my neck was permanently affixed to a 60-degree angle. I also lost my right ear to gangrene. To add insult to injury, my family didn't have insurance to cover the two-million-dollar hospital bill. But that's just a fraction of my story.

More than 36 years and 35 surgeries after the burn, I can easily point to any moment of my life and know it happened for a reason. From the day I was born (when my dad had to borrow money to pay the hospital bill) to being attacked by a bear to nearly drowning in whitewater rapids, nothing has happened to me by chance. I truly believe it was all with divine purpose that God was preparing me for something greater.

> **"**
> More than 36 years and 35 surgeries after the burn, I can easily point to any moment of my life and know it happened for a reason.

Many have trouble comprehending my ability to make light of my circumstances, but I learned early on that if you can't laugh at yourself, life is pretty miserable. Symbolism, humor, and clarity are always there if you look for them. You'll see these patterns demonstrated throughout my journey.

A kid who was derided as "Freddy Krueger" from Wes Craven's *A Nightmare on Elm Street* after the burn, I used self-deprecation and humor as a device to make others more comfortable and developed a charisma that landed me incredible job opportunities later in life. Though I was raised in a low-income, blue-collar environment, I worked my way to the top as a successful businessman. And I've also been lucky enough to encounter the joy of all joys: marrying the love of my life and having five wonderful kids together.

Through the many setbacks I've experienced for more than 40 years, what I've learned is that every obstacle is a great opportunity in disguise. Adversity defines champions. I've experienced firsthand how grit, perseverance, raw determination, and the refusal to quit can bury any obstacle. When situations get challenging and on the verge of a crisis, this is when I shine. I've programmed my mind to block out the noise and focus on the task at hand. After a lifetime of overcoming unfathomable situations, my success can be boiled down to three strategies:

> **"**
> Symbolism, humor, and clarity are always there if you look for them. You'll see these patterns demonstrated throughout my journey.

- Training my brain

- Shaping my reality

- Doing the daily things

I constantly look for people to tell me I can't do something so I can prove them wrong. I hope you're inspired to approach your life in the same way after reading this book. I hope you realize you have the strength inside you to rejoice in your sufferings, even in the most unimaginable ones. Adversity is constantly preparing you for something awesome, but you must have the faith to keep pushing forward even when everything inside you says to quit.

If you've ever encountered a challenge, this book is for you—whether it's the loss of a loved one, diagnosis of a major illness, being bullied at school, or just feeling like your life has no purpose. Whatever you're going through, you cannot stop fighting, no matter what!

Whatever plans you have, God has a different one. It's how you respond and adapt that makes you a great competitor. You can't plan for it all, but you can commit to doing whatever it takes to get through the hard times, resolve to keep your head high, and always laugh at yourself. Regardless of your situation, you can not only survive, but come out of the situation a stronger, better you. Move beyond the struggle and use it to find out who you really are and what you're capable of.

> **"**
> I hope you're inspired to approach your life in the same way after reading this book. I hope you realize you have the strength inside you to rejoice in your sufferings, even in the most unimaginable ones.

Embrace all that life throws at you. Celebrate the bad with the good. That's what I did, though I could have never known, as an eight-year-old engulfed in flames, how rewarding my life would become or what exactly that fire would ignite.

WHAT IS IRONMAN?

IRONMAN is the grandfather of all triathlons. It is a 2.4-mile swim, a 112-mile bike ride, and a 26.2-mile marathon run, all completed under 17 hours. IRONMAN is an extreme test of willpower and mental strength as much as it is of physical fitness. Every year, over 90,000 athletes vie for the coveted 2,400 slots to compete at the IRONMAN World Championship, referred to as "Kona" by insiders: the most prestigious endurance race in the world. To qualify for Kona, athletes must earn a slot by placing highly in their age group in one of IRONMAN's global qualifying races. Ever since Julie Moss crawled across the finish line of Kona on live television in 1982, the race has garnered the admiration of viewers worldwide.

Finishing an IRONMAN under 17 hours is tough, but I've never wanted to just finish anything. I want to be competitive and finish under 11 hours. It's particularly difficult when you have burn scars covering over 65 percent of your body, you're not able to sweat on one-third of your body, and can't quit sweating on the other two-thirds. To finish, you have to tap into reservoirs of will power you

WHAT THE FIRE IGNITED

never knew existed, recite to yourself limitless inner mantras and dedicate more than 10 hours a week to training.

To be competitive in IRONMAN, you learn how to do everything in motion—from eating to monitoring your heart rate to peeing. Having a perfect race is rare; so much can go wrong in a race over 140.6 miles. It's in these moments you must stay calm, put one foot in front of the other, and never give up. Never.

PART I

THE UNIMAGINABLE

IRONMAN World Championship

Kona, Hawaii

My day began early, with the canon firing at 7:00 a.m. to kick off the hallowed IRONMAN World Championship race. I had just completed a 2.4-mile swim and it was seven hours into the race. It was a day I had dreamed of since high school, but never imagined would be within reach.

I admit, it was a slow swim—1 hour and 23 minutes—followed by the 112-mile bike ride, which was easily the windiest course I have ever ridden. On the road to Hawi, we encountered 40-mile-an-hour crosswinds, nearly blowing me off the bike. As I pedaled, it was insanely hot, I was suffering, but I kept reminding myself, *this is Kona, the world championships—this is what you've dreamed about your entire life.*

After leaning on my aero bars of my Trek bike for five and a half hours, I couldn't wait to get off. But I was also about to start a marathon, a 26.2-mile run through a lava field. During the run, at mile 16, we would turn off the infamous Queen K and enter "the Energy Lab," an indescribable bowl of heat claiming the highest levels of solar radiation ever reported on coastal US.

Not one to make excuses, it's worth pointing out that I am unable to sweat on over one-third of my body due to the burn scars, and I can't stop sweating on the other two-thirds, making me extremely vulnerable to dehydration in hot races and urinating blood after every IRONMAN. The enhanced dehydration also causes my stomach to bloat and swell.

True to form, at about mile 90 on the bike, my stomach physically shut down, and I couldn't take in any solid foods whatsoever. I had already digested more than 10 GU energy gels (liquid food), felt pretty good, and was ready to start my run. With the bloating, I felt gas building up in my stomach and I thought to myself, *Man, I can't wait to pass this. I'm gonna feel like a new man.*

As I was running, I could feel it; here it comes. I passed gas and realized something: *Crap; that wasn't gas. That was something else!*

I tried to convince myself it was only sweat I could feel inside my lime-green spandex race pants—at least I hoped so. I was only half a mile into the run, and there were 26 miles to go. And all I could think was, *I am that guy. I've got a big, brown spot on the back of my pants, and it's going to be broadcasted on NBC.*

Off on the horizon, I spied a porta-potty, so I sprinted down the road like a man on a mission. Inside my safe haven, I discovered that my little accident was not as bad as I'd feared. However, full-blown diarrhea began to set in, which was less than ideal—particularly when running through a lava field.

In IRONMAN, you often have to think on the fly. I adjusted my run strategy and made a plan to run as fast as I could from porta-potty to porta-potty, which are spaced out at every mile. Every stop brought instant relief.

With 132 miles completed, I arrived at the gates of hell, the Energy Lab. I immediately located the porta-potty only to find it was … occupied. I waited impatiently for a few minutes. Finally, I started banging on the door only to realize someone had fallen asleep in there. It was so hot that the person in there had become dehydrated and literally had passed out sitting on the toilet.

Coming out of the Energy Lab, I felt like a changed man—the heat and desolateness had hardened my soul. I tried to eat a salted soft potato and threw up several times—my body was in full shutdown mode from the severe dehydration. I knew my suffering would only intensify. In full stride my entire body locked up in cramps. I collapsed to the pavement and lay there briefly telling myself, *Relax, you got this. Just get up. This is your dream.* I stood up and resumed full race pace only to lock up in cramps again half a mile later and every mile thereafter. With only seven miles to the finish line, I dug deep and fought back the tears as I high-fived my wife Brooke, the kids, and my good friend Feeney on my way to the finish line.

Believe it or not, that was my fastest marathon split in an IRONMAN race: 3 hours and 41 minutes with an official finish time of 10 hours, 45 minutes, 49 seconds—a respectful time, since I had only been competing in triathlons for three years.

After all I went through to get there, crossing the finish line was surreal. After nearly 11 hours at work, it's hard to imagine the race will ever end. At times, you really don't want it to end; you don't want to lose that feeling—complete euphoria, being on top of the world, like anything is possible.

As I undressed to go to bed that night, I surveyed the damage of the race on my body. I was peeing blood, and my skin felt like it was about to peel off. I was severely sunburned from nearly 11 hours in the lava fields. I was advised not to use sunblock, as it would make my sweating issue even worse. The bottoms of my feet were covered in blisters. The excessive sweating also caused every square inch of my body in contact with another piece of skin to rub raw. I thought I had carefully applied body-chafing cream to everything, but unfortunately the skin was even rubbed raw on both testicles, the back of my neck, both armpits, and part of my butt. Yet I felt it was all completely worth it.

> **"**
> **I always remind myself I'm so lucky to have the opportunity to test my mental and physical limits.**

I always remind myself I'm so lucky to have the opportunity to test my mental and physical limits. Who would have thought, as an eight-year-old kid lying in a hospital bed for two months and told I've never be competitive in sports again, that one day I'd be racing the world's hardest one-day endurance event—and not only would I be racing it, but I'd be competitive, finishing in the top 50 percent of the world's best? But it's not just the race itself that's so rewarding and exhilarating—it's the journey to getting there.

My journey to becoming an athlete worthy of IRONMAN was a long one, and it began when I was a kid. When I got out of the hospital, I truly believed the only way to get people to look beyond my scars and see me for who I am was to become an athlete. From that point forward, I had a new mission in life. I wanted to live for something bigger than myself.

I knew I wasn't the same kind of athlete I'd been before the fire. I had lost so much of my natural abilities. Discovering IRONMAN was a God thing. Unlike any other sport, it's not who's the fastest; it's who slows down the least. Anyone can be competitive for one or two hours, but let's put them out there for 10 to 11 hours in a lava field—let's see how they do with that.

Getting burned, years of rehab, over 35 surgeries, and continuous major setbacks prepared me for this event. This was the perfect sport for me. So how did I get to this moment? To understand that, you must understand where I come from. It's not a pretty picture, but it's what shaped me.

CHAPTER 1

To Light a Fire

> *If you're going through hell, keep going.*
> *—Winston Churchill*

t's hard to imagine three minutes of one day as an eight-year-old could change your entire life.

August 4, 1982, age eight. The day started like any other, hot and muggy—typical summer weather in Atlanta. My mom was between jobs and at home with me. The previous day, she'd helped me retrieve my bike, covered in yellow jackets, from my neighbor's yard. Mom was beginning to clean the house when she told me, "Now's a good time for you to go over and tell Mr. Smith[1] about those yellow jackets in his yard."

---

1   This name and that of the daughter have been changed to protect their identities.

I recruited my buddy Jeff Brown, age seven, for some neighbor-hood exploration, including a quick stop at the Smith house. Neither of us had any idea this would be the last time we step foot in that yard.

We set our bikes down at the bottom of the steep driveway, walked up, and knocked on the door. Mr. Smith wasn't there, but his 15-year-old daughter "Becky" was. I told her about the yellow jackets, and the three of us walked down the driveway to inspect the nest. There was a visible hole in the ground where yellow jackets were flying in and out of their nest. Recalling what she had seen her dad do just days before, Becky asked if we'd help her get rid of them.

"What do you want us to do?"

"I don't need you to do anything except stand here to make sure they don't leave the nest."

We did as we were told and stood there watching the yellow jackets flying around. Becky struck a match and threw it on the hole. Nothing happened. The match only flickered.

Jeff and I stood beside each other on the opposite side of the driveway, careful to keep our distance as we didn't want to get stung by the yellow jackets. The next thing we knew, without a word, we felt something splash us. It hit me on the right side of my body, splashing my shoulder, neck, and face. At the same time, it splashed Jeff on his left side.

We didn't even recognize what *it* was until it hit the still-flicker-ing match, and *whoosh*, we were engulfed in flames. *Gasoline!*

· · · · ·

The right side of my body and face were on fire, but for some reason I was still terrified of being stung by the yellow jackets, so I ran across the street to my yard to put out my flames. Recalling the lessons learned from watching the TV show, *Code Red*, I stopped, dropped, and rolled to put my flames out. Then I noticed Jeff was still over there screaming, completely consumed by flames. Instinctively I ran back across the street and up the driveway, grabbed the water hose and put the flames out. I continued hosing us both down with water, alternating between the two of us. The cold water provided temporary relief, but I had to share it every five seconds with Jeff.

I still remember holding the hose with my right hand and positioning it on our heads, letting the water pour down our bodies. We were completely blackened, our skin falling off, our clothes melted to our bodies. I remember touching my head and my hair coming out in my hands. We could smell the charred flesh. As I looked at Jeff, I couldn't recognize his face. *What just happened?* Our bodies were burning from the inside out. Words can't describe the radiating heat, and the burning wouldn't stop. The pain got worse with every passing second.

Mom was mad at first. The neighbors heard us screaming and told my mom we'd been burned. She looked out the front porch, saw two blackened kids jumping up and down and asked, "Where is he?"—not realizing those two kids were Jeff and me. She couldn't comprehend what was happening—she thought someone had burned a hand.

She was alarmed and angry and came running out of the house, assuming I'd been playing with matches. When she saw me there with a hose she went, "What did you do? What did you do?" And all I could say was, "Mom, I don't even know how to light a match." Mom realized then and there this was not of my doing.

The neighbors called 911 for ambulances to be sent. Somehow the dispatcher misheard and only sent one ambulance instead of two.

Not realizing just how badly we were injured, Mom let Jeff go first, because she knew he was burned worse than me. We had to wait another 10 minutes for a second ambulance to come and take me to Grady Memorial Hospital. My skin continued to burn. Once inside the ambulance, they immediately doused my body in saline solution to stop the burning. I cried looking out the back of the ambulance window, all alone and reflecting on mom saying "I love you" as the doors closed.

Mom walked back inside the house and called my father and made plans to meet at the hospital. When they rushed through the ER doors on the stretcher, no one was there to comfort me and assure me all was going to be ok—I was frightened, confused, and in shock. Making matters worse, my parents were prohibited from seeing me until early the next morning.

Mom really thought when she arrived at the hospital they were going to put Band-Aids on us and send us home. The doctor tried to explain to her, "Your life's going to change. This will not get better for years, if not decades." And she said, "So, you're telling me we're not going home tonight?" The doctor continued to try to explain the severity of the situation, but Mom didn't realize just how bad it was until she saw my body swollen three times its normal size. And to add insult to injury, lawyers were in the hallways, aggressively advocating for my parents to enlist their services to make the neighbors "pay for what they did." Although they had homeowner's insurance, their carrier was not offering to pay for our medical expenses. My parents were adamant: "How can we even think about suing them?"

• • • • •

Though I was numb with disbelief of the events occurring at that moment, I vividly remember being rolled into the operating room and placed on a table next to Jeff, surrounded by a team of nurses and doctors. I recall hearing the nurses frantically calling for different equipment as they tried to remove the clothes melted to our skin; every tug felt as if they were pulling off a pound of flesh. I remember them sticking us repeatedly with syringes to start IVs, voices calling out our vitals as they assessed the extent of our injuries. They tried to talk to us, get an idea of exactly what happened. They asked the same questions over and over: *How old are you? What is your name? Where do you live?*

I remember Jeff screaming uncontrollably, an indescribable pain in his voice adding to the mass hysteria. Still in shock from what happened and trying to make sense of the new surroundings, I summoned every ounce of strength I had left trying not to scream. I did my best to stay quiet, since the scene was already complete chaos—a room filled with total strangers in blue gowns and masks. All I could see was their eyes. *What did I do wrong? I was just standing there watching the yellow jackets. Mom is going to kill me.*

I had no idea what was happening, why it was happening, and if it would ever end.

. . . . .

Unbeknownst to me it wasn't until 1:00 a.m. or 2:00 a.m. the next morning when they finally rolled me out of the operating room and into ICU. I lost all conception of time. I felt I had been on the operating table for days. Everything was a fog. Nothing I had experienced before had prepared me for this.

For the first four days after the burn, I was solely fed through a tube in my nose and given no liquids. I thought it was a luxury when I was finally able to start sucking on ice chips ... progress.

I've learned since then that everything is relative. It would be over a month before I was able to return to solid foods.

Severe burns are followed by severe stress, inflammation, increased metabolic rate, and increased core-body temperature. It's common for the liver to increase 225 percent in size, heart rate to increase 160 percent, and overcall cardiac output to increase 150 percent. There is also a major loss of lean body mass as skeletal muscle is used to fuel the body. To offset the increased metabolic state, more than thirty thousand calories a day were pumped into my body through the feeding tube. Burn trauma has an unfathomable impact on the body. The swelling of my entire body was beyond comprehension. Dad vividly recalled my hand being bigger than his—an eight-year-old kid's hand bigger than that of his father. And that hand was not even burned, except for my thumb.

> **Dad vividly recalled my hand being bigger than his—an eight-year-old kid's hand bigger than that of his father. And that hand was not even burned, except for my thumb.**

Using my left arm, I slid the food tray holding my ice chips forward, allowing the mirror underneath to flip up. I screamed uncontrollably at the reflection in the mirror. *What was this monster staring back at me?* Hearing my gut-wrenching screams, hospital staff stormed the room while two attendees secured me to the bed while another sedated me. The screams faded as I drifted into sleep.

What I saw didn't resemble a human face, much less that of an eight-year-old boy—much less the face I had seen in the mirror just a week before. It was swollen, contorted, still blackened with red all over, wounds still very fresh. My head was double its normal size.

I couldn't believe this was me. This was not some horror movie; this was me. *Would I look like this forever?* This was the image flashing in my head when I closed my eyes to go to sleep.

EAR DIARIES PART I:
CHOCOLATE EAR

Getting a prosthetic ear was a whole new experience. Imagine having everyone see you with only one ear for the past 26 years. I walked into Dr. Davis' office for the last step of the process. The previous month he had casted my right ear and somehow made an inverse copy to be used as my new left ear, but only a fraction smaller. Supposedly, making it a bit smaller forces the brain, subconsciously, to focus on the ear that is a little bigger. He snapped the left ear, cast out of clay, onto my head and passed a mirror and cautioned "Don't focus on the color, the final version will be made out of silicone and hand painted to match." As I looked into the mirror, I now saw I was perfectly balanced with two ears ... only one was chocolate brown because it was made of clay. I immediately asked Dr. Davis to take a photo with my cell phone. Anxious to share the good news, I posted on Facebook: "Major News!!! What do you think about my new ear? I got this one half off." From the picture I posted, it was extremely obvious my new ear was not a good match. It was dark chocolate brown compared to the pasty white of my right ear. The comments immediately began pouring in, "Dude, how much do you need to get the matching version?"

IRONMAN Florida

Panama City, Florida

With every race, there's always something unexpected. The key is to just embrace it. Something weird will always happen, and you can only do so much preparation. In the end, you just have to embrace the chaos.

My first IRONMAN competition ever was in Panama City, Florida in 2009. That was also my very first year doing triathlons; I'd only been in the sport for six months, but had somehow managed to successfully prepare for my first IRONMAN in that timeframe.

I was in great shape, and I had almost my entire family—including my dad; my sister, Britney; Brooke and our two kids (we were just getting started with our brood); plus my mother-in-law, Marilyn; her parents, Joe Cat and Yogi; my wife's Aunt Vin and Uncle Mike—there to support me. And, oh yeah, my good friend Donald Stretch and his wife Christy were also on hand. I felt like a celebrity with my cheering section.

This one was like all race mornings. In my race-morning routine, I get up at 4:00 a.m., eat pancakes, (I aim to eat three hours before the race starts), drink coffee, and my body goes through its normal processes. Everything was great. But 30 minutes before the race started, my stomach got extremely upset from nerves, so it was off to the porta-potty for me—happens every race.

All of a sudden I noticed there's no toilet paper. What was I going to do in this predicament? There's no way I could hold it for an 11- to 12-hour race.

Desperate times call for desperate measures. I shined my phone light around and noticed inside the actual toilet itself a huge wad of unused toilet paper. Yes, I did. I reached in, dry heaving, and grabbed it, and I was able to use enough to get out of the bathroom. Such relief! I headed to the start line feeling like the weight of the world had been removed from my shoulders. I had the best swim I've ever had in an IRONMAN race.

During the bike ride I came upon a rider at mile 40, and this guy was a lot bigger than I am: height, weight, everything. We all have our names on the backs of our bibs, and I like to talk to people, as I pass them. So I say, "Hey, John, you're looking strong, man. How about you loan me those legs?" He had huge quads. He looked over at me, laughs, then he grabs his belly, shakes it and goes, "You gotta take this with it; it's a package deal."

I laughed. I had to keep pedaling up. Then at mile 75, I came across a woman rider. The swim was a mass start and we're four and a half hours into the race, so I'm thinking, "This woman has put it to me. I'm just now catching up to her." I said, "Hey, Cindy, you're looking good." She peeked back over her shoulder and pedaled faster and pulled away from me. I was like, "Oh, crap. What is she doing?"

The ego kicked in. I started pedaling a little faster, and then I looked down at her calf—you've got your age on your calf—and this woman was 49—14 years older than I was, and I said to myself, "No way I'm getting beaten down by a woman almost my mom's age, even if I have to rest in transition to recover." I pedaled harder, pulled ahead, and I told myself, "No matter how bad this hurts, you can't slow down."

I made it to the end of the 112-mile bike ride to see my family cheering and still holding the sign "Ride it like you stole it." I was re-energized. I had a great run, finishing in a total of 10 hours, 31 minutes and 15 seconds. I finished in the top 12 percent of finishers: my first IRONMAN in the books.

After talking with other IRONMAN athletes, I had set a finish time of 12 hours as my goal with a stretch goal to finish in less than 11 hours—and to come in at 10 hours and 31 minutes, I was beside myself. I was ecstatic, and of course kept thinking, *Man, what could I do if I had a better bicycle? What if I actually knew what I was doing?* It's the *what ifs* that always drive me to work even harder and set my goals even bigger. Dream big!

Chaos Beyond Comprehension

> *It is better to aim high and miss than*
> *to aim low and hit.*
> *—Les Brown*

Take a deep breath. Walk around the room before you start this chapter. Part I is like competing in an IRONMAN. Chapter 1 was the grueling swim where you're fighting for your life and constantly reminding yourself to stay calm despite being kicked and pinned under water. Chapter 2 is the long bike ride, the longest part of the race, a mental endurance test where you think it will never end and emotions run rampant. Chapter 3 is the (almost) impossible feat of *a marathon, where the name of the game is put one foot in front of the other and just run one mile 26 times.*

The experience mirrored my life during and after the fire. For weeks and months after the burn, I was confined to a hospital bed and thought it would never end, one complication after another. Then for months and years after being discharged, I was back at school, adjusting to my new life and struggling to find my identity. The only way I could survive was just how I run a marathon: one mile at a time, one day at a time.

By the end of Part I, despite still carrying the burden of my scars, you'll see my life was starting to come full circle—graduating both as senior class president and a competitive wrestler. As you can imagine, that and so much more fueled me to embrace the chaos.

The initial days after the burn involved continuous monitoring and assessments of my condition to determine the treatment plan. As doctors walked Mom and Dad through the litany of surgeries and months of treatment and rehabilitation the injury entailed, they learned the bill would easily surpass $2 million. Mom said, "I don't want to buy the hospital. I just want you to fix my son." And the doctor said, "No, ma'am, that's what it's going to take to get your son back." We didn't have insurance and the Smith's homeowner's policy was denying liability. Dad had lost coverage on dependents when he'd switched jobs to work for Mom's dad—and they were barely making ends meet as it was.

News spread quickly through church prayer groups and eventually to the Shriners. The Shriners immediately called and offered to treat me at no cost at the Shriners Hospital for Children in Cincinnati, Ohio (500 miles from our home in Decatur, GA). Despite their generosity, Mom had to think on that one, because honestly, she didn't want to move to Cincinnati and be all alone. She was diagnosed as manic depressive and had long abandoned her prescribed lithium. Her episodes only intensified with new environments, and everything she knew was in Atlanta. My dad couldn't go—he was the only one with a job. But with no insurance, we had no choice but to accept their enormously generous offer. The Shriners would cover all costs, if only we would come to Cincinnati—so we did. Mom recalls this moment as a critical point in her life. She sat down on the floor in the hallway at Grady and just cried, repeatedly asking God, *What do you want from me? Why me?* Within her she could feel a calming voice telling her to make a choice. *Are you going to be selfish and live for yourself or are you going to live for your son?*

Within four days, the Shriners sent down a private plane, adequate but small. Mom panicked. She has a fear of flying and, to make matters worse, is claustrophobic. She refused to get on the plane. She had already prepared herself for the move, but this was another curveball, not one she was prepared to handle. Ever accommodating, the Shriners agreed to get her a seat on a commercial flight and have her meet us in Cincinnati.

I still remember being pushed across the tarmac, strapped to a gurney, and loaded in the plane. There was barely enough room for me, the pilot, and an attending paramedic. Oddly enough, this was my first time on a plane—too bad I couldn't look out the windows. All I could see was the blue sky and white of the clouds as we climbed to our cruising altitude. Jeff would join me at the Shriners, even though he had insurance to cover his medical bills.

We're Not in Kansas Anymore

Once we got to Cincinnati, Mom settled into a boarding house of sorts, a dorm room setup for adults with four twin beds in each room, four rooms to a floor, and just one bathroom on each floor. The main floor contained a community kitchen, dining room, and living room. There in the common space everyone had to watch the same TV show. Imagine the setting for a hospital ER waiting room minus the sick patients. This was Mom's new home for the next three months.

There were very set times for visitation and when visitation ended, everyone would go back to the dorms and attempt to decompress and block out the day's events. For Mom, it was bad enough to be in her thirties, alone, 500 miles from home, and sharing a room with three strangers, but these roommates were parents who were extremely stressed out, each going through the same thing but dealing with it differently.

Dad was lucky, in a manner of speaking, in that at least his job kept him preoccupied and somewhat distracted from what was happening 500 miles away. He didn't have to relive the nightmare daily and see the pain in my eyes. There's nothing that prepares a parent for when his or her kid is suddenly in a life-or-death situation. Not surprisingly, Mom's roommates had their own habits and coping mechanisms—one would stay up until late hours, one would talk on the phone nonstop, and one would constantly take smoke breaks. The stress was unbearable; Mom's manic depression spiraled.

Within a week of me being in the ICU in Cincinnati, my dad delivered a huge box stuffed with cards from my would-be classmates—third grade started without me. Suspended above me from chains from the ceiling was a large piece of plexiglass. The nurses quickly placed all the cards and hand-written notes on the glass, so I could read them while lying on my back—a position I would spend more time in than I care to remember. Shortly after the cards from my classmates arrived, I received autographed photos from Herschel

Walker (Heisman trophy winner; I was a huge Bulldogs fan growing up), William Andrews (All-Pro Falcons running back; I'm a Falcons fan for life) and Dale Murphy (consecutive MVP winner; the Braves player every Atlanta kid pretended to be in the backyard). I still have no clue how they heard about my story. As I lay in my bed staring up at their photos, I wondered if I'd ever be able to play football and baseball again. I dreamed of the day I'd one day lace up my shoes and compete again. I made a pact with myself that once I got out of the hospital I'd do whatever it took to compete again.

> As I lay in my bed staring up at their photos, I wondered if I'd ever be able to play football and baseball again. I dreamed of the day I'd one day lace up my shoes and compete again.

It's odd the things you remember, or forget, or choose to block out. One of the first things I distinctly remember upon being admitted to the Shiners Hospital is having my head shaved with a lady's leg razor. I also recall overhearing the doctor explain to my mom that there was a strong likelihood my growth would be stunted. In burn trauma, especially at a critical growth age, the body will divert calories needed for growth to focus on repairing itself. Turns out, I indeed grew to be considerably shorter than the six-foot projected height that had been based on all my previous growth charting.

No Pain No Gain

To understand burn trauma in 1982 is to imagine a time when they didn't believe in induced comas. They didn't believe in morphine.

It was believed if you were screaming, your lungs were healthy. The strongest thing administered to us for pain was Extra Strength Tylenol. I can still recall the fear of daily dressing changes, you'd hear the entire ward erupt with kids screaming. Even an hour beforehand, I'd dread it. You'd know it's coming. And unlike school or work, we didn't get the weekends off for good behavior. For debridement, I was placed into a metal tank—"the tank"—where they would scrape and scrub me with a wire brush to remove the dead tissue. Just being wheeled to the tank room required every ounce of courage not to cry in anticipation of the pain to come.

I was originally diagnosed as having 35 percent of my body burned, with a projected discharge date of six weeks. Unbeknownst to the doctors, though, I was extremely susceptible to infections and keloiding, which is excessive scar-tissue growth. Infection is prominent among burn patients and is one of the largest causes for complications, and I was no exception. The constant rotten stench of the infection is ingrained in my brain. Even today I am highly sensitive to the smell of sinus infections.

As it happens, I lost my first three skin grafts to infection. Wasted and irreplaceable. A skin graft is when the doctors harvest healthy skin, the top two layers (epidermis and part of the dermis), from one part of your body (donor site) to replace the damaged/burn tissue. Initially, skin was harvested from the tops of my thighs to graft to my face, neck, shoulder, and arm. Unfortunately, I had a double whammy—the grafts got infected and didn't take, and they had harvested the skin from my thighs too deeply,

> **"**
> If there's a 1 percent chance of something going wrong, I'm usually in that 1 percent; history has reinforced that.

essentially making them third-degree burns and requiring skin grafts themselves. As a result, once all surgeries were completed, I went from being burned on 35 percent of my body to having more than 65 percent of my body covered in scars. I have never encountered anyone else who had to have a donor site skin grafted to—if there's a 1 percent chance of something going wrong, I'm usually in that 1 percent; history has reinforced that.

Human Quilt

Thirty-six years later, my body could be called a human quilt. Pieces of my legs, back, stomach and butt have been removed and placed elsewhere. Much like a quilt, each square of skin has its unique markings and story. When all was said and done, I had all the skin harvested from my entire right leg, all the way from hip to ankle; from my left leg, hip to knee; half of my back; my right buttock; and a three-by-eight-inch section from my abdomen. Petting a skin graft on my right cheek, friends jokingly tell me my face is smoother than a baby's butt—knowing it came from my butt.

I'd be remiss if I didn't share some of the other joys of skin grafting in 1982. Each time a graft was performed, I was immobilized for five days. No movement whatsoever—I did everything lying in bed—eating, going to the bathroom, brushing my teeth. As painful as the skin grafts were, the heat lamps used to heal the donor sites were even worse. The donor sites were basically raw, open wounds that required heat to promote healing. A 40-watt heat lamp was placed 18 inches above my legs and turned on for 20 minutes of every hour for the first few days of the process. Each session of the heat lamp triggered memories of the fire; my legs felt like they were on fire, and no relief of the pain was available. Sleeping was inconceivable with these lamps cooking my legs.

The skin grafts were secured in their new location with staples. I had staples in my legs, face, neck, back, shoulder, arm, stomach, and even inside my ear. It's hard to imagine, but in 1982, the staple removal tool consisted of the same staple remover you'd find in any office or classroom. As each staple was removed, my skin was pinched as the metal teeth were slipped under the staple. The staple removal process took several hours, and to pass the time, I counted the staples as they were removed—more than 50 in each leg.

Ear Today, Gone Tomorrow

Unfortunately, the infection wasn't limited to just my skin grafts. During the same time, my right ear, severely burned, had become infected and gangrened. At first, the doctors were very optimistic, thinking it was salvageable. Visually, it looked like burned s'mores and the smell was overwhelming—I was scared to ask if others smelled it for fear it meant they'd need to cut it off. Every two days, the attending doctor would make his rounds for assessments. Almost without fail—and without painkillers—he'd take surgical scissors from his lab coat and trim off the corners of my ear until it bled. The pain was immense but like everything it would pass, and the doctor would assure us the bleeding was a sign of healthy tissue. After a few weeks of holding out hope, they finally concluded the gangrene was spreading and could potentially seep into my head, so the ear had to go.

They broke the dreaded news to my mother first and asked whether she wanted to tell me the bad news or if she preferred they do so. She insisted it should come from her. She tried to stop herself from crying as she broke it to me in a way that was courageously cheerful: "Shay, I need to tell you something important. You see your Dad over there?" she asked, pointing to him as my eyes were fixed on her. "You see those big goofy ears he's got? You are so lucky. You are only gonna have one of those." And that's how I found out I would have my ear amputated. Humor has played a huge part in my healing. If you can't laugh at yourself and life in general, you're going to be miserable.

I accepted this loss more easily than is probably normal, but, honestly, my ear amputation was the least of my concerns compared to everything else I was dealing with. A month had passed, and I still couldn't use my right arm. My arm had melted to my body and formed a webbed affect—the skin melted into a thick band of scar tissue under my armpit. Physically lifting my right arm was an impossibility. The skin had no elasticity and was permanently stuck at a 45-degree angle. To remedy the band of scar tissue, they would cut the burned skin, remove more skin from my leg and staple it in, essentially giving me an extra two to three inches of skin to work with. With my entire upper legs previously harvested, they decided to use the skin from my right calf.

My right arm was completely bandaged for the first two months. I did everything left-handed, from brushing my teeth to feeding myself to using the bathroom. Even today there are many things I still do left handed, like changing diapers (Brooke swears I'd do a better job if I'd use my right, but it just feels natural). The Shriners were very big on, *You can do it. We're not here to take care of you.* Tough love is what we needed, although the screams may have indicated otherwise.

New Normal

It took three years and multiple surgeries for me to lift my right arm up over my head. During that time I had to wear a full-body, custom-fitted compression suit to minimize keloiding. It was in two pieces, Velcro securing the two halves, and went from my ankles, to my neck, and all the way to my wrist. In addition to the compression suit, I had to wear three custom plastic orthotic braces: a side brace, a neck brace, and a face mask. The side brace went from my navel up to the middle of my chest, around to the middle of my back, all the way up under my armpit, and it extended down to my elbow. The brace was molded to secure my arm at a 45-degree angle; to soften the scar tissue, I'd strap the brace as tight as I could stand it until the skin turned white from the pressure.

The plastic neck brace extended from to the top of my chest up to my chin, stopping right up under my ear and down to my shoulder blades in the back, covering the tops of my shoulders in the front. My neck had the same webbed effect as my armpit, permanently stuck at a 60-degree angle. The neck brace would be reshaped as my range of motion improved with each surgery.

Lastly, I had to wear a plastic face mask, essentially a hockey mask, with holes cut out for my eyes, two holes cut out for my nose, and then a slit for my mouth—but it was clear. It also had a little beanie cap with Velcro straps to tighten the brace. In total, I had to wear the compression suit and all three orthotic braces for 22 hours a day for three years, only taking them off to shower, eat, or exercise. Decked out in my new equipment, I was an instant eyesore everywhere I went. Having my body stuck in these positions with constant pressure was extremely uncomfortable and at times just outright painful. The worst was trying to sleep with everything on. No amount of pillows provided a good night's sleep.

I remember crying myself to sleep at night for months. I prayed for God to heal me. I asked my parents to please make it go away. Nothing. No amount of crying, praying, or pleading eased my pain. I hated it, all of it—not the least of which was having to wear the compression suit and the three plastic braces everywhere I went. I wasn't angry, just frustrated because there was nothing I could do; I felt helpless and all alone. There was no one to talk to and I definitely didn't want to be a burden. Who could even pretend to understand what I was feeling, physically and mentally? It didn't take a genius to figure out no one looked like me—I didn't belong in my new environment.

Everywhere I went, people stared. I can't say I blamed them. I had never seen anyone like myself before being treated by the Shriners. The staring was tolerable, but the comments were unbearable. Other times they didn't need to say a word, you could see it in their body language, in the shame in their eyes, their unwillingness to hold eye contact with you. That's the thing; it's not just the scars. You adapt to physical pain, but the mental pain is a constant reminder you are different and all alone.

Mom did her best to dismiss the stares we received in public. She'd say, "You may not look good right now, but those kids are gonna be ugly the rest of their lives. Your scars will get better." A part of me believes Mom was saying it to also convince herself.

I Didn't Have It That Bad, Really

One thing I learned quickly is regardless of how bad your situation is, someone else has it worse. Despite everything I've endured, I'm the lucky one. There's not one thing in life that I've ever missed out on. Did I have to work five times as hard as everyone else to get the same opportunities? Absolutely. But guess what? It meant 10 times more to me when I achieved my goals, because I had worked so hard. When you've lost everything, you celebrate the smallest of victories and never take anything for granted. You also realize happiness is a mind-set.

The company you keep has a big impact on your mind-set and perception of reality. Fortunately for me, I was initially surrounded by kids who were burned far worse than me, but their attitudes said otherwise. Once you meet these kids and hear their stories, you'll see why I felt lucky and why their attitudes made me realize I didn't have it so bad after all.

Jon-Jon, just two years old had the only crib in ICU. He was in his garage when he somehow pushed over a gasoline container, which rolled under a hot water heater, blew up, and he found himself covered in fire.

Then there was a teenager named Travis. His accident occurred while his father fueled up their boat at a marina and somehow it—and Travis—blew up.

At some point, a guy named Eddie was rolled into our room and parked next to my bed. He was 17 and had lost half his leg and half of his foot from installing a TV antenna on a roof. He and his brother hit a live wire, which killed his brother and basically killed all the tissue in Eddie's leg and foot. Eddie introduced me to *MAD* magazines, *The Benny Hill Show, Welcome Back Kotter,* and *Taxi.* Yes, I was just eight, but I grew up fast. Eddie pretty much controlled the remote.

Toward the end of my stay, there was a guy brought into my room with 90 percent of his body burned. His mother's boyfriend set the house on fire while he was asleep. I don't recall his name, but he was severely burned and had no eyelids. No nose. No ears. Just little nubs for fingers. At night he would freak me out because it always looked as if he was looking at me. He kept a pair of sunglasses by his bed and I assumed it was to aid in his sleeping. When he fell asleep, I would waive my hands over his eyes to make sure he was sound asleep before putting the sunglasses on him to help me rest, too.

Another kid was burned across his entire face and the top of his head, essentially permanently bald due to the severity of his scars. He did however have a small patch of hair that ended at the crown of his head. To address his situation, they inserted two tissue expanders, silicone bladders that were injected weekly with silicone, at the crown of his skull. During the expansion process, he had two large, softball-sized growths protruding from the top of his head. Because of the resemblance, many called him Mickey Mouse.

Lastly, I distinctly remember a smiling five-year-old girl, whose name I never knew, but I can still see her little face as she walked from room to room to say hello. Her story still resonates every time I see a kid with a cigarette lighter. This girl had grabbed her dad's lighter, and when she lit it, it blew up in her face, melting her face to her chest. She had no neck, no nose—just two holes and nubs for fingers.

I met a lot of great kids during my time there, kids who were far worse off than I. But when I went back in for my checkups, for whatever reason, I always felt I was different from these other kids. Their situations were direr, and I didn't see myself in the same boat as them. I just thought, *You're gonna be normal. These kids, man, they've got it really rough.*

Boy in the Mirror

When I looked in the mirror, I only looked at the left side of my face, completely ignoring the scars on the right side. Honestly, I didn't want to remind myself of the injury; I felt the more I could distance myself from being the "burn kid," the faster I could resume a life of normalcy. I believed if I acted like I didn't have the burns, others would treat me that way. I was determined to forge a new identify that had nothing to do with being a burn survivor. In fact, I don't and never have seen myself as this horrible burn victim, or "burn survivor." I've always seen myself as someone who had a bad accident, one of the many that would occur before and since. But, to me, accidents always imply you're getting better. It's something temporary—not something that will impact you forever or attach to you a permanent label. For me, labeling myself as a "burn survivor," implied there is a permanent mental and physical deformity, something that will over-shadow anything else in life I overcome or achieve. I never wanted special treatment; I abhorred it. All I wanted was to be treated like everyone else. I want to be remembered as a man of God, a husband, a father, a man of passion, a fierce competitor, and someone who made a difference in the lives of others. Not for some accident.

EAR DIARIES PART II:
EXTREME BODY SCANS

It was Friday night at 5:00 p.m. and I was in Hartsfield—Jackson Atlanta International Airport. I still had to get through security, and it was one of those excruciatingly long lines. As I scanned the lines, the room was filled with tension as travelers wanted to be anywhere but there, myself included. So when it came to me I thought, *You know what? I'm gonna have some fun.* I took my right ear off, and I put it in the tray with my shoes and my cell phone. But I also had a backup ear, because every three years I get a new one—these things wear out. I took my backup ear out of my briefcase, and put it in the tray, too. Without hesitation, through the scanner goes my shoes with my cell phone and not one, but two right ears.

All of a sudden I saw the guy working the scanner stop the belt and glance at the screen with a perplexed look. He stood up, and he looked around kind of like, *Who's punking me?* He advanced my tray through the scanner again, stops, then he rewound it. Meanwhile, I just went through the scanner, but all he saw was the left side of my body, completely obscuring all the scars on my right side. So, after four times, he was just completely exasperated and at a loss—he went ahead and advanced my things through. I reached in, grabbed my ear and snapped it back on. I shot him a thumbs up, and he just started shaking his head …

Training for Beach 2 Battleship Iron Distance Race

Atlanta, Georgia

IRONMAN required as much mental training as physical training. I was a big proponent of training outside and training to race-day conditions, regardless of the elements, and without headphones—imagine a seven-hour workout with no stimulus whatsoever. Weekends were my big training days, with Saturdays including a six-hour bike ride and one-hour run off the bike, all without headphones and by myself.

Mental toughness separates good athletes from great competitors. In 10-plus years of IRONMAN training, I've never done a long run with anyone and only one long bike ride with someone; it's always just me and my thoughts. I am always looking for everyday experiences to sharpen my mind, especially when traveling for my job. When making three- to four-hour drives by myself, I often turn the radio off and just drive in silence. It's amazing the thoughts that go through your mind when you remove all unnecessary distractions.

I even took one memorable 50-mile bike ride in the dead of winter while it was a bone-chilling 17 degrees outside. It was so cold all my water bottles froze within 30 minutes.

To prepare for the lava fields of Kona, I heated a room in our house to 100 degrees, layered up in a sweatshirt, thermal underwear, sweat pants, and gloves and did a one-hour workout twice a day for the three weeks leading up to the race. I nearly overcooked my grits when I did an eight-mile run in 109-degree heat with thermals (June 29, 2012, hottest day on record in Nashville[2]) and almost didn't make it back home.

My use of mental training techniques were also utilized one particular winter while training for my second IRONMAN race, the Beach 2 Battleship Iron Distance Race in Wilmington, North Carolina.

It was late October, and to prepare for the race, set for three weeks later on November 13, I decided to do a two-hour bike ride outside at the same time I anticipated coming out of the water from the swim. I knew race day would be a chilly one, in the low forties. It was 8:30 a.m., 37 degrees, and I was dressed in my normal race kit: spandex biking shorts, a sleeveless racing top, and a pair of arm warmers. Train like you race. That's it.

I spent the next two hours riding at race pace along the Silver Comet Trail, a train rail converted to a bike path from Atlanta all the way to Alabama. Speeding down the path, I passed walkers and joggers wearing hats, gloves, and ski jackets, and there I was in a tank top and shorts. They looked at me like I'm crazy, and I kept telling myself, *Hey, it's not too bad. You're actually pretty warm. Just imagine what it'll feel like on race day when you come off the bike and you're in the top 10.*

I flashbacked to Coach Pritz, who always had multiple one liners, like *Pain is temporary.* Or, *Pride is forever.* Then there was, *Pain*

---

2   "Nashville Weather Records (1871-Present)," National Weather Service, accessed August 10, 2018, https://www.weather.gov/ohx/otherrecords.

is weakness leaving your body, or, *No guts, no glory,* and, *We pray for overtime, because that's when we thrive.* It's all these reminders that when the going gets tough, that's when we shine. Meanwhile, I was chattering, and this is what I endured for two hours to convince myself it wasn't that cold, when actually, I was freezing! Eventually I told myself, *No one is stupid enough to do this. If you can do it and survive, the race will be nothing.*

Before long I realized I basically had hypothermia. Once in the car, it took me 45 minutes to quit shaking, even with a sweatshirt, jacket, and toboggan cap on, with the heater at full blast.

> **When the going gets tough, that's when we shine.**

Later on I found out that in the race, people would definitely be wearing jackets and windbreakers, but that's just another thing I learned the hard way. As with a lot of things in life, I learned about IRONMAN intricacies through trial and error.

It turned out that I finished second in the race. It was my best finish ever and it reinforced to me that we should always rejoice in our sufferings, even when our teeth are chattering and we're frozen from the inside out.

CHAPTER 3
Sink or Swim

Tough times don't last; tough people do.
—Pastor Robert Schuller

Returning to school after the accident was surreal. The accident happened the month I was meant to begin the third grade, but instead of a seamless return with the rest of my classmates, mine was extremely unsettling, filled with stares, whispers, and who-knows-what behind my back.

For the previous 10 weeks, I'd been in a very controlled environment. Everyone was either going through the same thing I was—scars all over their bodies, missing body parts, fully bandaged—or supporting their child who was going through the trauma with us. Everyone at the Shriners was accustomed to seeing burn scars and disfigurations. But once I walked into school, I was no longer in a controlled environment. To say I stuck out like a sore thumb is an understatement.

The doctors warned us about this at the hospital, but no one can really prepare you for what awaits when you begin the transition back to some kind of normalcy. We were advised to take a few months to get used to the real world before I returned to a classroom, but my parents believed we had to deal with it as soon as possible—I'd already missed two months of third grade. With only a two-week break between the hospital and school, boom, I was back: back to the books, and back to confronting reality outside the hospital room.

Getting dressed for school was something I couldn't do alone. I was still wrapped in bandages, and I wore the three braces as well. I could only wear polo-style shirts, as my neck and arm wouldn't move enough to allow me to wear a normal T-shirt. I had trouble walking because I'd been bed-ridden for two months. When I walked, I didn't have a normal gait; my legs couldn't fully bend and extend as before. Everything about me caught the attention of others, and in every hallway, people stopped to stare or whisper, and some just turned their head in disgust. Even though the school tried to prepare the student body for my return and urged them to support me, kids still couldn't help being kids. Nothing they had seen could prepare them for this—no one had seen a picture of me, and they had no idea what to expect. The last image they had was of a handsome eight-year-old who excelled in sports … not some kid strapped to orthotic braces. I remember it like it was yesterday, the silence that fell upon every hallway whenever I turned a corner. Regardless of what people were actually saying, I felt it was always about me.

And then there were those I could hear. I learned very quickly that kids can be cruel. Shortly upon my return, the Wes Craven movie *A Nightmare on Elm Street* came out, and it got to where kids would pass by and say, "Hey, Freddy"—as in Freddy Krueger. For the first few months, it really got to me. When I looked in the mirror, that's what I saw. I saw Freddy Krueger and kept thinking, *God, what a horrible monster.*

But after a while, I realized that of course I am not a monster. I just happened to be in a bad accident. There was nothing that could fix the scars, so I decided to have a little fun with these kids and started responding to the Freddy comments with, "Yes, and I'll see you in your dreams tonight." That put an end to that joke pretty quickly.

During this time, because of the number of open wounds I still had that were bandaged, sterilization was very important—keeping the wounds clean was a major undertaking. I bathed twice a day. Mom had to pick me up every day at lunch, take me home, give me a whirlpool bath, treat me with Neosporin and Nivea cream lotion, rebandage me, put my braces back on, and take me back to school to finish the day.

As if that wasn't challenging enough, during my first week Mom locked her keys in the car. The only thing she knew to do was to ride the 10-speed bicycle from our home two miles to the school to pick me up. I didn't have the strength to walk or bike home, so she propped me up on the seat and pushed me and the bike all the way home. Despite the challenges, I stayed on track and got straight As. Finishing third grade with my friends was a major accomplishment, especially because I had to do it all left-handed, since my right arm was of no use.

Despite all the challenges, I still managed to find joy in little things. For nearly a decade I thought my right nipple had been burned off; I never could see it when I lifted my right arm to look. Then one day I was standing in front of the mirror and raised my right arm. Low and behold I found my nipple. It was up near my collar bone. The scar tissue was so tight on my neck and shoulder that it pulled my nipple up every time I lifted my arm. Hmmm, what a nice surprise.

Sports And I, Still A Pair

Sports have always been part of my life, playing organized baseball at age five and football at six. Getting back into sports played a major role in my healing, mentally and physically. Even though I couldn't be competitive, sports gave me a sense of belonging and feeling normal—well, almost normal. At first it was hard accepting the fact I would no longer be picked first on the school playground. I was now picked last with the other nonathletes. But at least I was given a chance to compete. Independence was a major part of my healing.

I always told myself, *The scars will never go away. It's something I can't hide.* But I truly believed if I became a great athlete people would overlook the scars and just see me as an athlete, not the burn kid. I played baseball just two months after returning home. I played second base because it was the closest to first base. Throwing was challenging due to my right arm's limited range of motion, but I managed to throw the ball side-armed. I couldn't slide into bases due to my open wounds, a disability one opposing coach took advantage of in a game. A situation arose where a pinch runner was needed on third base, and the opposing coach had the option of selecting, and he chose me, knowing I could barely run and couldn't slide. As soon as he did, my mom became unhinged and charged the field screaming at him. Rules are rules, but Mom sure gave him a piece of her mind.

Once baseball season ended, I played football just two months later. Football was a major risk as I had no nerves, sweat glands, or fat tissue on my right shoulder and arm. Doctors did not support me playing, fearful I would suffer a major hit and seriously damage my shoulder without any padding protecting my bones—or worse, I'd sustain a cut and bleed out without ever knowing (you can stick a needle into my arm and I won't feel it). To remedy the doctors' concerns, Dad inserted additional padding into my shoulder pads, doubling the protection.

Injuries and playing through the pain has been a major part of sports for me. Never one to heed caution, I made an ill-fated decision to go skateboarding before a baseball game. Naturally, I fell off and broke the same wrist I'd broken when I was six. Fearful of disappointing Dad, I played the game with a broken wrist although Dad was suspicious in pregame warmup. I had been able to bat both left- and right-handed ever since getting burned, so I batted left-handed in that day's game and actually got a hit. Fielding infield grounders was a challenge, but I managed. After the game we went to the doctor and, sure enough, I'd broken my left wrist again.

Reinvention Can Be Salvation

Whether consciously or subconsciously, I've always taken advantage of moving and changing schools as opportunities to reinvent myself. After the fourth grade ended, we moved to Marietta, Georgia as Mom finally secured new employment. It was a fresh start in many ways. New neighborhood, new school, new friends, a chance to recreate my identity—a chance to not be known as the "burn kid."

After we moved, I never saw Jeff or Becky ever again. It's been 36 years and counting. As I got older, I prayed for Becky. I prayed she not carry the burden of her actions and that she really never know everything we endured. I made several attempts to contact Jeff via the Shriners and former classmates, but I was unsuccessful. Last time I saw him, he had healed up nicely. His scars actually looked much better than mine.

Fifth grade was like starting over, because no one knew my story and I didn't volunteer it. I felt like I came in with a clean slate. Don't get me wrong, people still asked and stared, but because I was two years past the injuries, I wasn't handled with kid gloves. My appearance was still a head turner—I could still hear comments, but for me the big change emotionally was just being in a different environment.

Wrestling with Change

The progression to middle school was another life-changing moment. I'll never forget walking into the school and seeing a poster on the wall that said, "Join the wrestling team." I loved WWF, the wrestling I saw on TV, and I was like, *You mean we can do this as kids? That's awesome.*

I begged my dad to look into it, and he did. We got to the first practice and I quickly found out: this is not WWF. This is collegiate-style wrestling. There are rules, there's no body-slamming, no figure-fours, and there are no ropes to bounce off. But we did we wear those awful one-piece singlets. I soon realized this was my calling. This was a sport where the playing field was level, and I was competing against other kids who were within five pounds of my weight. When I played football, I was always the smallest guy on the field. Always. I was the shortest, weighed the least, and was the slowest—not favorable attributes. In wrestling, though, it doesn't matter how tall you are or fast you can run—it's how much pain you can handle, how much pain you can dispense, and for how long. Coach Rollie Lambert invested extra time in me. A spark plug of a man himself, he helped me channel all my pent-up emotions into competing on the mat. I really excelled because my pain threshold was unparalleled. By the time I finished the eighth grade, I was voted the most valuable wrestler. When I stepped on the mat, I was a different person. I was not your friend. I was aggressive and attacked you like I was shot out of a cannon. I wanted nothing more than to wipe the mat with your face. I wanted to inflict pain and give you just a taste of what I endured every single day. Coach Lambert's confidence in me allowed me to embrace my new identity. No longer did I have to hide my scars; I could now wear them with pride.

Going into high school, I had a newfound confidence. I'd already talked to Coach Gordon Pritz, McEachern varsity wrestling coach, a legend in the making, and he expressed interest in me being part of the team, even inviting me to work out with the team that summer after middle school to get a head start. This moment catapulted me into sports. My whole life all I wanted was for someone to believe in me and I'd run through walls to reward their trust. I'd been competing in baseball and football, but when high school came along, I had to choose. I was still doing three sports and requiring ongoing surgeries, so I had to give up the sport least important to me to schedule surgeries in the offseason. Regrettably, I let go of baseball—in retrospect I was better at it than football. I held onto football a little longer, because I loved it so much and believed my Daniel "Rudy" Ruettiger work ethic would pay off. Wrestling was really the only sport for me. It's almost like my burn injuries had prepared me to excel on the mat as a competitive wrestler.

The thing about sports and I is that, after getting burned, I kept looking for ways to deflect all the attention from the scars and channel my pain. I really felt if I became a great athlete people would not focus on the scars. But my athletic abilities didn't show up in my earlier performance. There was nothing in fourth or fifth grade that would make anyone about-face. But when I was introduced to wrestling, my talent started to come out in a you'll-have-to-kill-me-to-beat-me mind-set. My ability to take and inflict pain helped set me apart from others; I started gaining recognition through wrestling. Most of all, I felt I belonged.

> **My scars continued to give me an edge in wrestling. I really believed they intimidated people, or at least that's what I told myself. I envisioned my opponents thinking, *You know there's nothing I could do to him that hasn't already been done.***

My scars continued to give me an edge in wrestling. I really believed they intimidated people, or at least that's what I told myself. I envisioned my opponents thinking, *You know there's nothing I could do to him that hasn't already been done.*

GROWING PAINS

One major setback was that as I grew, my burn scars didn't—skin grafts and scars don't have the same elasticity as normal skin. In the ninth grade, the scar bands on my neck became unbearable, pulling down the right corner of my mouth and eye and cutting off my hearing when I turned my head to the left. To remedy this, the Shriners inserted a tissue expander in the left side of my neck. A tissue expander is a silicon bag, essentially a breast implant, inserted underneath the good skin, and it's inflated with weekly injections of saline into a port to stretch the good skin.

Once fully stretched, the excess skin would be used to replace my burned skin. I was not a fan of more skin grafts—and we'd seen miraculous success stories and truly believed this procedure would fix all the burns on my neck. As soon as my freshman wrestling season was over, the tissue expander was inserted into my neck and blown up over six weeks with weekly injections. The softball-sized expander was extremely uncomfortable. My skin felt taut and like it would rip open at any second. The large growth sticking out of the left side of my neck presented a popping hazard, plus it garnered unwanted stares: perfect for a freshman in high school.

The doctors believed, based on how large the expander was inflated, they'd have six to seven inches of new skin to play with. Once the expander was removed, however, my skin only stretched half an inch. They'd never seen this before, and now I had an incision mark from my left ear to my right ear and back to my left clavicle.[3] In the end, I endured complete hell for two months all for nothing and with more scars than I had before the surgery. I expected to awake after the surgery and see unburned skin on my neck and no more nagging scar bands. I was completely devastated to see I was not only wrong but worse off than before the surgery. I didn't blame the Shriners; it wasn't their fault—it was due to the fact that I easily keloid, and the fact that I am, again, *always the 1 percenter.*

By the time I finished my wrestling career at McEachern High School I was a three-time region champ, finishing second in state my senior year, and setting the team record for the most wins by pin. I was projected to win state, but two weeks before the state meet, I was diagnosed with a nasty virus, which caused diarrhea and vomiting. I was so sick I could not hold down food for two weeks and was seven

---

3   Bizarrely, mysteriously, and hilariously, this scar would start the rumor at school that I'd been nearly decapitated in a motorcycle accident.

pounds under my normal 125 weight for the tournament—I was severely dehydrated to say the least. My tongue was so swollen I couldn't keep it in my mouth. I was so drained I had to forego warming up before matches to conserve energy. The goal is to always go into the match already sweating—you never walk on the mat cold. I breezed through my first four matches, but each match took a toll, and I lost in the state finals as a result. I had dreamed of this moment my entire middle and high school career and was devastated it ended this way, knowing if I had been healthy the outcome would have been different. I eventually came to terms with it but always felt I had unresolved business—some things go wrong, no doubt, and this experience would serve me well leading into IRONMAN.

> **No one stared at me because I was freakish—all eyes stayed on me because I had something to say.**

By the time I finished high school, the same kids who 10 years earlier ridiculed me as "Freddy Kruger" elected me senior class president.

As president, I spoke confidently to our senior class at graduation about seizing this moment, not taking anything for granted, and going out into the world to be our best selves—I went from feeling next to useless on a baseball field to being a wrestling champ, from a kid hiding under bandages to a guy with his head held high, speaking at a podium in front of a sea of people. No one stared at me because I was freakish—all eyes stayed on me because I had something to say.

IRONMAN Dream Begins

As a child, I had watched IRONMAN on TV and dreamed about what it would be like, racing through the lava fields and being a part of something bigger than life. One summer while at a church youth camp in Panama City, Florida, my buddy Chris Caldwell and I came up with our own IRONMAN event at the camp—though it was nowhere near the length of the real race. In our triathlon, we swam the length of the pool and back. With no bikes available, we navigated an impromptu obstacle course through the camp, and then finished up with a half-mile run. It was just a taste, but it was great, and I was hooked.

IRONMAN was one of those things we just fantasized about. I never really thought, "Hey, one day I'll be doing this." I had never even met an IRONMAN. It wasn't until 2009 that it became a reality for me, following college and many more pivotal life events.[4]

EAR DIARIES PART III:
ALWAYS CHECK THE TRAY

During my junior year at McEachern High School in Powder Springs, Georgia, we flew to Blackwood, New Jersey for what's called the Best of the Best Wrestling Tournament. We were the Southeast powerhouses and defending state champions in Georgia.

If you know anything about wrestling, it's a grueling sport and the weight-cutting causes as much pain as the rigorous conditioning. I had been cutting weight for this tournament and

---

4   No one could have foreseen that Chris's brother Matt would one day be one of
     my big Kona sponsors.

so had everyone else.

On the plane, we were served lunch, and I ate part of it before going to the bathroom, only to come back to find the stewardess had taken my tray and disposed of my meal. Like a lot of people, when I'm cutting weight, I'm moody and fussy, so I said, "Hey, ma'am. Are we gonna get more food? I notice my tray was taken." She goes, "Oh, I took it away. I'm sorry but there's no more, only one per person for the plane." I said, "Oh. Did you happen to see my ear on the tray when you took it? I'm kinda gonna need that."

She looked and saw I had no ear, and was instantly mortified. Without saying a word, she ran to the back of the plane, and we saw her talking to another stewardess. Next thing you know, they'd turned the trashcan over and were digging through it, frantically looking for my ear. All of my wrestling buddies were just dying laughing. Coach Pritz overheard the laughter, came over and said, "Eskew, you oughta be ashamed of yourself." I said, "Coach, she shouldn't have thrown my tray away. I was hungry." He went back and told her it was all just a really bad joke.

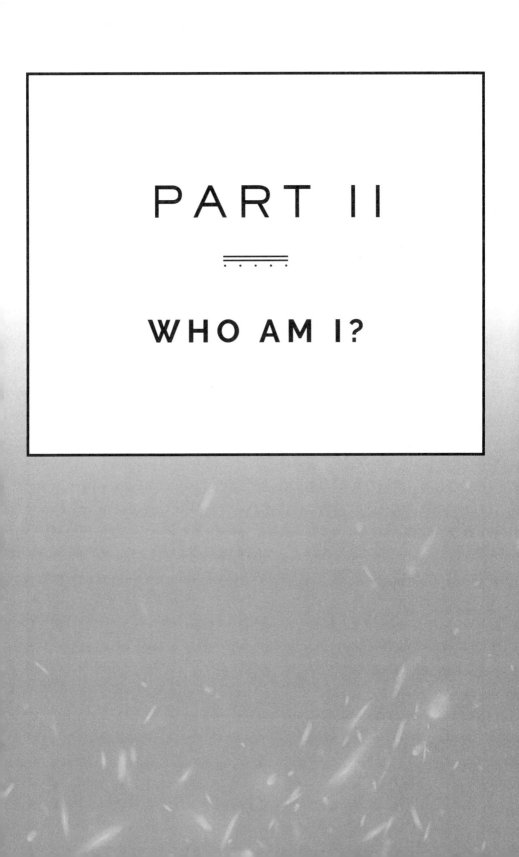

PART II

WHO AM I?

Beach 2 Battleship

Wilmington, North Carolina

Beach 2 Battleship was my second IRONMAN race, and my second season competing in triathlons. One of the things I'd realized by this point is that in order to be fast, I needed to shave off every minute that I could, however I could. That meant learning how to pee while riding a bike. Yep, you heard me right. Race friends told me I was wasting three to four minutes, at least, stopping at a porta-potty. And because trying something new on race day is not recommended, I had to practice. Yes, I decided to practice peeing in motion.

During a few long, 120-mile bike rides, I tried to pee, but I just couldn't do it. No matter how badly I had to go, I physically could not pee on myself.

Next thing I know, it's race day. I was about 60 miles into the 112-mile bike ride and alone out there—no one in front or behind me. I had to go, so I thought, *This is it. Do it. Be a man.* It took about five minutes before I finally started peeing; I was super excited: This was what I'd been working for! I used my extra water bottle to squirt myself clean. Relatively speaking.

Once off the bike, I ran through a gallery of people in downtown Wilmington, where I managed to pick out my wife. From 20 feet away, I yelled, "I did it! I did it!" Brooke high-fived me, but my parents were confused. "He just peed on himself!" she told my mom, who then asked, "And we're celebrating this why?"

CHAPTER 4

College Years and Daredevil Days

> *Everyone has a plan until they get*
> *punched in the mouth.*
> —*Mike Tyson*

D eciding where to go to college depended first on where I could wrestle, but eventually came down to affordability. At the University of North Carolina at Chapel Hill, we met with the coach and discussed my accomplishments and team needs. He expressed interest in me joining the team as a walk-on; he had already filled all scholarship positions but seemed enthusiastic about getting me into the school. I even stopped by the bookstore to buy a sweatshirt and hat. But when we got home, Dad said the tuition was not something we could afford. The same thing happened when visiting with Duke, so we didn't even go through the formal admissions process. We learned we had waited too late to secure a wrestling scholarship—like a year too late. It was down to a choice between the University of Tennessee (UT)—Mom graduated from there and they offered me an academic scholarship—or the University of Georgia (UGA), which is where I finally decided to go. It was close to home, in-state tuition, and I had a lot of friends there. Also, I'd be close to my then-quasi girlfriend in Atlanta, which backfired on me after she dumped me three weeks into the school year. But that wasn't my only UGA setback.

My major was architecture, and UGA only offered an engineering program. I'd planned on taking core classes and eventually transferring to UT, only to discover UT required architecture classes from day one—a major oversight, but one of many through life that helped me find my way. I did end up transferring to UT after the first quarter, but not before more obstacles further confirmed Athens was simply not the right place for me. Having missed the deadline for securing a dorm, I lived off campus and never really felt like I was a part of the school.

The Greek system dominated campus life at UGA, and Mom, who was in a sorority in college, thought it'd be something I'd enjoy. "You'll meet some of your best friends," she said. I went through formal rush and had two of my high school buddies go through it with me. The process was a bit overwhelming but there was one fraternity I really liked. And I thought they liked me.

When it came time for bids, however, I didn't get a single one. I was so distraught and in disbelief. How did I go from being senior class president and a well-known wrestler to not even getting a single bid? Rejected, yet wanting an answer, I stopped by the fraternity house I really liked. One of the guys I hit it off with gave me the heartbreaking news. "I hate to be the one to tell you this," he said, "but I feel like you need to hear the truth. It was a close vote, but several of the guys thought your scars might be an issue."

Who would have thought something as silly as scars and no ear would keep you from getting into a fraternity? But it reinforced what I faced my entire life: that's how the world works. A lot of people judge a book by its cover, and the people who voted against me had formed an opinion strictly based on my scars. This was not the first time I encountered being an outcast because of the burns; it was just the first time someone actually told it to my face.

College was supposed to be a place, I thought, where you would find where you belonged, and that was not the case here. I was neither building new friendships nor was I working toward my architecture degree. At the end of the quarter, I packed my bags and made the move to UT, starting my first semester in January of 1993.

Big Orange Country

As soon as I got to Knoxville, it was snowing, as if the heavens were sending a sign: *Welcome, Shay. Here's your clean slate.*

Now *this* was everything I had envisioned. I lived in a dorm and quickly met what would turn out to be some really good friends. And though I was behind on architecture, I took higher-level elective classes, made great grades and was on the dean's list every year I was there. I even took advantage of the extracurricular activities and joined the water ski team and the mountain bike club.

As a sophomore, UT felt like home and things really seemed to be turning around for me. Eager to make a fresh start, I tried the greek scene again and pledged Lambda Chi Alpha, a diverse group of guys who embraced everyone. One look at the Fraternity Composites told the story. These guys weren't the typical pretty boys; there was something unique about them, plus they had the reputation of being the fun guys. Truly, this is where I met the best friends of my life.

By 1995, I was living with my fraternity brother and good friend Brian Feeney in an old, beat-up, rundown house that had been divided up into multiple apartments. My late-night ritual to burn off stress included a bike ride through the city by myself: no lights, no helmet, just me and the darkness of night. Albeit not the smartest thing, one of the things I loved to do was mountain bike through campus, descending down the iconic concrete stairs of "The Hill." For me it was just a release; I truly felt like I was alive—the right balance of adrenaline and fear.

One particular night I biked out to the 1982 World's Fair site. The last thing I recall is riding down the concrete stairs in the little amphitheater. The next morning I woke up in my bed with the word "Tuesday" on my right hand. I had no recollection of how I got there. Feeney told me I came home late the night before claiming I hit my head. Suffering from a concussion and short-term amnesia, I kept asking what day it was—hence he wrote "Tuesday" on my hand—and took me to the hospital. The hospital thought I was on drugs, because I kept flexing my bicep as they took my blood pressure and growling as I murmured, "Get you some." Feeney assured them, "Trust me, this guy is completely drug-free."

My daredevil escapades continued throughout college, and looking back, it's a miracle I survived. I was convinced God had bigger plans for me and would take me when he was ready.

Eye of the Tiger

My hallmark at UT was boxing in the Sigma Alpha Epsilon (SAE) Boxing Tournament. This is not your normal collegiate boxing tournament. The event takes place every February and attracts more than 10,000 attendees over a three-night period. With wrestling a foregone memory, I missed competing and desperately needed something to train for. Once I heard about the tournament, I knew it was perfect for me.

To enter the tournament, you had to go through training, get signed off by a Golden Gloves-sanctioned trainer and prove you could protect yourself. I entered the tournament three times and won it all three years. I never lost, and was even inducted into their Hall of Fame. Renowned trainer and Knoxville icon Ace Miller, who'd trained Olympic gold medalist Evander Holyfield, took me under his wing. Ace told me, "You are never going to find someone out there who's tougher than you are. You remember that." That was just another reminder for me that it's not about being a great athlete—it's about being a great competitor. His whole point was: These great athletes get punched in the mouth, and everything goes out the window. People like you, that just gets you fired up.

> **"**
> Ace told me, "You are never going to find someone out there who's tougher than you are. You remember that."

Going into the tournament I knew I wasn't the most skilled athlete. But one thing I did know was no one would train as hard as I did. I have never lost a sporting event because I wasn't in shape. I've always done the hard training. Talent was something outside of my control, but physical fitness was well within my control. Taking a punch and coming back for more doesn't come natural. Most people try to avoid getting punched in the face. For me, getting hit was inevitable. I made sure I could take a hard punch by the best. I always sparred people in higher weight classes, sometimes 30-50 pounds heavier. I believed if I could take their punches, the guys in my weight class would be a breeze. When I sparred, I sparred to win. I wanted to make sure if any of my potential competitors were watching they knew what they were in for. All of my sparring partners will tell you the tournament was easy for us, because we beat the crap out of each other in practice.

The draw of the tournament included local celebrities, city officials, and a significant portion of the UT student body. At one tournament, I met Peyton Manning, the school's future NFL Hall of Famer. He found me in the crowd and made it a point to come speak to me. One of the advantages of my scars that's been reinforced over the years is I definitely stand out. When I stood in the ring, everybody in the whole crowd could see all my scars, and I guarantee it made me unforgettable.

One of the things I told myself during training was, *You can't afford to lose. The only way you're ever going to get a date on this campus is if you win. If you lose, no girl will ever go out with you.* And whether right or wrong, I convinced myself losing was not an option. I clung to boxing for dear life as the way to a girl's heart. I could never have known then the woman I was going to marry couldn't care less about my boxing titles. Turns out she was more impressed with my German Shepherd, Harley. Go figure.

The 15-Year Divot

I started college at a whopping 135 pounds and, after hitting the weights hard, ballooned to 155 at the end of my freshman year. Unfortunately, as I grew, my grafted skin didn't. My right arm was at least two inches smaller than my left due to the extensive skin grafts not accommodating my growth, essentially acting as a tourniquet. After several years of losing circulation in my arm during exercise, I returned to the operating table at Shriners for more surgery on December of 1995, this time to try to address my right arm. Basically, they made an incision from the top of my shoulder all the way down to the inside of my elbow. The incision caused an immediate release of 2 ½ inches, creating a huge divot in my arm. They reharvested skin from my right thigh to fill in the huge void, resulting in a massive depression that measured two fingers side-by-side. They also cut my neck and allowed it to release over two inches, sewing in skin taken from my hip. Familiar with the drill, I scheduled surgery a week before Christmas to prevent interfering with school.

The hospital experience was beyond miserable. Although the pain was manageable, the inability to move whatsoever was intolerable. I had to lie flat on my back for seven days without a pillow and with a hole cut in the bed for my head. To preserve the integrity of the skin graft, I wasn't allowed to move my neck, or anything for that matter, for those seven days. It was torture. I'd rather take a beating in the face than have to lie still for that long. I did everything lying on my back: eat, drink, and going to the bathroom. Little did I know the embracing of discomfort was molding me into an IRONMAN.

When I was out of the hospital, my parents had to bathe me for the first two days. You talk about embarrassing—when you're a twenty-one-year-old having to get your parents to bathe you, it's pretty humbling, to say the least. I could see the tears in my parents' eyes as they witnessed their son reduced to this condition.

When they removed the dressing from my arm, I was not prepared for the huge depression where the incision had been made. I was speechless as my eyes teared up. I was mortified with the thought I'd have to walk around the rest of my life with a huge divot in my arm. My dad placed two fingers side by side in the divot and they were swallowed up by the huge depression. Every year, a little bit more of my arm would fill in. I took over fifteen years before people finally quit asking what happened when I took my shirt off. Eventually, I couldn't help myself and told everyone I was attacked by a shark.

Rocky Mountain High

If you don't know by now, I never let a good obstacle go to waste. I know every obstacle is a blessing in disguise and my surgery in 1995 was no different. I'm always about maximizing experiences and believe my surgeries afforded me permission to do something bold. After the surgery I had to wear the old plastic neck brace again for 22 hours a day for three-to-six months. I knew from the start I'd be tempted to not wear the brace when I was with my friends. An opportunist, I convinced my parents to let me transfer somewhere totally different for the following semester, some place where I'd feel more comfortable, where I wouldn't know anyone and be tempted. Another clean slate.

By this point, I'd already become disillusioned with the prospect of being an architect after hearing I'd probably spend my first 10 years drawing closets and bathrooms. I decided to turn my attention to something else I loved, where I wouldn't be so inhibited: wildlife biology. And since Colorado State University (CSU) had the number one wildlife-biology program in the country, and access to great snowboarding, that's where I decided to spend my semester away from Knoxville. I even managed to talk Rob Gilmore, adventure partner and fraternity brother as well as future godfather to my oldest son, Maddox, into joining me, although he didn't need much convincing. We had been roommates in the fraternity house for the past year, and he was buying time for nursing school to start with no immediate plans. I thought, *Why not drive out with me and lets see if we can find you some temporary housing?* Upon showing up on campus we learned I hadn't been assigned a roommate and decided Rob would be my new roommate—a miracle from above. We made it three weeks before he finally got busted for living on campus and not being a student, but boy did we have fun. We were both even able to live off my student meal plan. (I'd sneak food out in my pockets). Rob took a Greyhound bus home shortly after.

Colorado was great—when I wasn't snowboarding in Breckenridge or skiing in Telluride, I would go mountain biking, with my sights set on the mothership of mountain biking: Moab, Utah. One weekend in Moab I earned a trip to the ER—a plate and seven screws later I was all patched up. That was a tough phone call home, not to mention undergoing surgery with no family there.

With my leg still in a walking cast at the end of the semester, my dad flew out to help me drive back to Atlanta—a road trip for the ages. We made it worth our while, hitting up the Grand Canyon, the Hoover Dam, Moab, and Arches National Park, stopping to camp

WHAT THE FIRE IGNITED

out every night, just my pops and I sharing a two-man tent. It was a treasured experience with Dad I'll never forget.

Bear-ly Surviving And Climbing ol' Rocky Top

Back home, I rested and prepared for my senior year at UT. My time in Colorado had a profound impact on me and made me long for the outdoors. I romanticized living off the land and adopting the lifestyle of a frontiersman. After graduating with honors (cum laude), one of my professors, world-renowned black-bear biologist Dr. Mike Pelton, invited me to be one of his research assistants—assisting his two PhD students—trapping black bears for research purposes in the Great Smoky Mountains. We caught more than 150 bears, the most ever caught in the over 20 years of the study. It was only a $75-a-week gig, but all I could think was, *Oh my God, who wouldn't want to do this? You mean I get paid to do this?*

I spent six months living in the woods—three months in Cades Cove, Tennessee and three months in the Okefenokee Swamp down at Stephen Foster State Park in Fargo, Georgia. Accommodations included a 40-year-old, beaten-down trailer with no air conditioner, no TV, and no screens in the windows, and only a rotary phone for emergencies. Oh, and no deodorant either—we didn't want to give off any scents to spook the wildlife. We killed 10 mice in the trailer the first week in the woods. And fortunately, another roommate who soon joined us was a five-foot long, mouse-eating rat snake—who we could hear slithering through the walls of the trailer at night. Bear trapping sounds glamorous, but we worked 14 days on and four days off, regardless of the conditions or whether or not you were sick. I had the distinct pleasure of wrestling with one bear during a torrential thunderstorm—lightning flashing across the sky every two seconds. Germaphobes take note: we never washed our hands during the 12 hours we spent in the woods daily, even after handling the bears, packing out their poop for a scat analysis or slaying a wild boar with just a hatchet. (We had a few get caught in our traps and they are a major nuisance animal to the park.)

But that was nothing: one day I was attacked by one of the bears. The other research assistant and I were working our trapline (seven traps covering a 10-mile hiking trail) when we noticed a bear was caught and not moving. We utilized a leg snare trap, basically a five-foot piece of quarter-inch aircraft cable, with one side of the cable attached to a tree that allowed the bear to run around the tree in all directions and the other end of the cable made into a cinching foot loop to ensnare the bear's foot. Our trap lured the bear to step in a designated spot, triggering a spring arm to cinch the foot loop around one of its paws. But this particular bear was tangled up in the cable, pinned up against the tree and in severe distress. We needed to sedate him quickly and feared he was hurt. Since a trapped bear is always agitated, sedating one of them is a two-man job: one guy distracts the bear while the other pokes it in the hip with a ketamine-filled syringe mounted at the end of a three-foot aluminum pole— then he quickly gets out of the bear's five-foot cable-limited reach. The drug takes about 15 minutes to work.

With the bear distressed and appearing immobilized, I encroached inside the five-foot radius by myself. There was no excess cable, because he was all tangled up in it. I immediately prepared the drug and, to make a cliché literal, poked the bear right in the hip.

I was within three feet and the bear was still motionless. As soon as I poked him, the bear moved, and I could then see he was untangled with five feet of excess cable. I didn't have time to turn and run. I backpedaled as fast as I could to get out of his reach, but my movement was impeded, and I was pinned against a rhododendron tree. The bear took two steps and leapt out with his two front paws extended and his mouth open. All of a sudden, I felt the sharp claws grab my left arm and start raking down its entire length. I started screaming, sure that my arm had just been severed from my body. The bear dropped to the ground, at the end of its lead. Still in shock, I looked down at my arm and saw that the bear had only ripped my shirt sleeve off, leaving three claw marks the full length of my arm. It was bleeding, but it wasn't anything that needed stitches. My partner heckled me saying, "You were screaming like a little girl."

In addition to that experience, other memorable wildlife encounters included the following:

- We were asked by the red wolf biologist to remove a black bear that somehow climbed into the wolf acclimation pen (30-foot square enclosure, 10 feet high). The other assistant and I jumped on the wolf that was inside with a cargo net and held him down while the PhD student chased the bear out of the pen.

- We caught a cub one day, and mama wasn't happy. The entire time we tried to sedate and release the cub, mama circled us, popping her jaws and huffing (forcibly blowing air out of her nose). The PhD student assured me "Ninety-nine percent of the time the bear is bluffing."

- I took my fraternity brother Jim Bencik on a hike, educating him along the way on what to do if we encounter a bear. Sure enough, I spotted one 50 yards off eating vegetation and thought it was a great opportunity to display how bears are afraid of humans. Unsolicited I yelled, "Hey bear, hey bear," hoping the animal would take off. The bear had other plans and ran at us full speed. I held my ground, making myself look as big as possible and repeatedly screaming, "Hey bear, hey bear." Eventually the bear ran off after getting within 10 feet and finally catching our scents.

After six months in the woods without the comforts of life and women (did I mention no women?), I realized I wanted more out of life—this was a hobby, not a career. I needed to make money, and I couldn't support myself doing that, much less, hopefully, a future family. Adventure was something I could satisfy through road trips and worldly excursions. My parents had always given me the advice of "Do what makes you happy," but in hindset I think they should have said "Do what makes you happy … and pays your bills."

I wouldn't take that experience back for anything, though. One of the themes in my life has always been about experiences. When I'm presented with an opportunity I know not many would take advantage of, I do it, whether its trapping bears or performing feats of strength in Morocco or living in a tent in the desert for two weeks. With this bear-trapping experience, I thought, *Why wouldn't you do this? Imagine the stories you can tell your kids and all your friends to say, "Hey, I lived in the woods for six months trapping bears for a living."*

As you'll see, my post-grad years have been filled with pivotal moments: meeting life-changing people, overcoming more difficult challenges, and, of course, finding all kinds of new adventures.

Road Trips and Near-Death Experiences

Like life, road trips have a start and an end, but it's the journey in between that makes the experience memorable. I truly believe we are often presented with two paths in life, and I have always chosen the one less taken. Anyone can book a vacation and do the usual sight-seeing exploration, but only the adventurous go off the beaten path and let opportunities unfold as they present themselves.

I have taken numerous cross-country trips, and all without making a single hotel reservation. I learned early, no matter how rough the trip starts off, you have to be committed to finish it and embrace whatever obstacles arise. If you haven't figured this out by now, saying yes to a great adventure is one of my biggest weaknesses. One road trip stands out in particular.

Nashville to Seattle, September 2000: My fraternity brother Brandon Barnes asked if I'd be interested in riding with him to Seattle as he made the journey back to Anchorage, Alaska. I met him at 4:00 a.m. to learn he'd met a truck driver at a wedding the night before who was driving to Sioux Falls, South Dakota. The truck driver had an empty flatbed trailer and agreed to let us hitch a ride with him and load our SUV onto his trailer—saving us a ton of gas money. Fourteen hours later, we parted ways and continued our road trip, sleeping in a tent on the side of the road near Mt. Rushmore before eventually arriving in Missoula, Montana. After grabbing pizza in a local restaurant, we continued pushing the pace through the night with Brandon behind the wheel. At 2:00 a.m., I was jolted from deep sleep by the sound of tires screeching as the SUV jerked a hard left. Brandon had fallen asleep. Still dazed, I saw a state park sign strike the front of the SUV; instinctively, I covered my head and ducked. The sign came through the windshield, narrowly missing my head. The vehicle then started flipping and we sailed upside down across two lanes of traffic and struck a tree 20 feet up in the air. We hit the tree so hard with the back end of the SUV, still upside down, that we landed back on our wheels. We were on a windy river road somewhere in Idaho with no cell phone coverage. We quickly assessed our situation. Brandon sustained a nice gash to his head and me a nice laceration on my hand and head. Brandon's head was much worse than mine as blood covered his scalp.

My *MacGyver* skills kicked in and I built a fire on the shoulder of the road using a Pop Tarts box, a *Maxim* magazine, and the splintered state park sign; (It had recently rained, and the local deadwood was soaked). An hour later, a semi-truck came by and radioed the state patrol, who in turn dispatched a local wrecker. Little did we know the wrecker was dispatched out of Missoula, an hour away. We assured the state patrol officer we were fine, just needed a patch-up at a doc-in-the-box. As morning broke, the wrecker loaded our SUV and took us back to Missoula, dropping us off at a car-rental facility.

Big forest fires in Missoula had depleted the rental car inventory, our only option was a 20-foot Ryder truck. With a new ride secured, we found an urgent-care facility where we got stitched up. We decided to spend the night in Missoula and set out early the next morning for Seattle. Still reliving the series of events in our mind and contemplating just how lucky we were, we decided to stop by the accident site to investigate the carnage, and I was hoping to find my CD collection that was thrown from the truck. As we walked to the spot where we struck the state park sign, we soon learned how close we came to meeting our maker. We were only a few feet from going off the narrow river road into a ravine with a 50-foot drop-off. Had

Brandon not corrected the vehicle, we definitely would have been killed. The gravity of the moment was not lost on us.

EAR DIARIES PART IV:
PLEASE DON'T FLUSH

After church one Sunday, we visited Panera Bread to grab lunch. My son, Beckett, had been complaining about his stomach hurting, but he seemed okay otherwise. As we were finishing our meal, it became clear he was truly sick. I rushed him to the men's room, carrying him with his head resting on my shoulder. We were standing in the stall, and all of a sudden, I heard a ferocious series of rumblings coming from his stomach—I knew what this meant. I tried to hurry and reposition him over the toilet as food began to exit his body, but I wasn't quite fast enough. Vomit got on the wall, the toilet, and the floor. During the course of the intense projectile vomiting, his arm dislodged my ear and knocked it into the toilet. There it was—my ear sitting at the bottom of a public toilet with chunks of grilled cheese and tomato soup floating above. I called Brooke on my cell and had her take Beckett to the van. With no other option, I rolled up my shirt sleeve and stuck my arm into the toilet to retrieve my ear. I washed it best I could in the Panera sink.

ITU World Championships

Las Vegas, Nevada

In my second year of racing triathlons, I qualified to compete on Team USA in the 2011 ITU (International Triathlon Union) Long Course World Championships in Las Vegas. I spent 10 months preparing for this race and was truly in the best shape of my life. I knew it was going to be a tough one; the course was regarded as the toughest long course triathlon in the world.

Brooke and I flew out there two days early to get acclimated to the desert-in-November weather. We expected 60- to 70-degree weather, but a cold front came through and temperatures plunged to the forties. Race day was expected to be in the thirties.

Race-day morning, I was pumped, despite the 37-degree temps. They cancelled the 4,000-meter swim due to the near-freezing conditions and made it a rolling bike start. I was elated at the news—they had just cancelled the hardest part of the race for me. Somewhat bummed that it was no longer a true triathlon, I was excited to know I had a shot to finish in the top fifteen. The course was my ideal profile: everything about it told me, *this is your race.*

For the first 10 miles on the bike, I was ecstatic, passing people left and right. I was on fire. Then suddenly at mile 10 of the 75-mile bike course, I got a flat—my first ever flat tire during a race.

I stayed calm and didn't panic. Within two minutes, I managed to change my tube out and was back at it, passing people who'd passed me while I was changing my flat. At mile 20, my front tire went flat again and, sadly, I didn't have a second inner tube. However, I did have another CO_2 canister. I pumped the tire all the way up and got back at it. But yet again, 10 miles later, it went flat again. The tube was faulty.

My buddy Butch Wabby rode by and lent me his CO_2 to keep me advancing. I got to mile 40 before it went flat again, so I decided to just keep pedaling on a flat tire in hopes of coming across the SAG wagon (support vehicle).

By mile 50, the tire washed out completely and I slammed into the concrete, cracked my helmet, and scraped up my hips and elbow—all in front of a huge gallery of people watching.

I was so jacked up on adrenaline, the only thing I could do was roar loudly … then I started laughing. Laughing is what I do when I'm in pain. Then it finally hit me. *God, I've always wanted to do an ultramarathon; I just didn't realize it was today* (an ultramarathon is anything over 26 miles). I still had 25 miles to go on the bike, followed by an 18.6-mile run. I couldn't run in the cycling shoes, so I took them off, along with my helmet, affixed them on my aero bars, and started running while pushing my bike. A spectator ran beside me and asked if I needed help. I gave him Brooke's phone number and asked, "Can you call this number? Her name's Brooke. Tell her I'm gonna be late, but I will see her at the finish line." The guy didn't believe me. He called Brooke and said, "Hey, your husband's out of the race. You'll probably see him before too long."

I was six miles into my barefoot run when I came across another cyclist who'd ripped his tire in half—but his tube was intact. He threw me his inner tube, but he didn't have a spare CO_2 cartridge for me. I put the tube around my neck and started running again. I got half a mile into the run again before a British girl tosses me a spare CO_2 cartridge. Not believing my good fortune, I changed the flat tire and quickly biked in the last 19 miles. I laced up my Newton running shoes—my feet swollen, bruised, and starting to bleed—and then I ran the final 30 kilometers (18.6 miles).

Quitting wasn't an option. Before I left home my five-year-old daughter Olivia said, "Bring me home a medal daddy." Her simple request played over and over in my head during those last eight hours of the race. I finished the race, and I still beat three other finishers. On the flight home I was commiserating with Brooke about the race and took comfort knowing no matter how tough it gets, I will always finish. I will never give up. Everything in that race said, *quit, you're not gonna finish.* But I stuck it out.

A week later, I was contacted by Rob Urbach, CEO of USA Triathlon. Rob was impressed with my perseverance to finish and offered to do a feature on me for their 2012 Olympic preview issue. I never could have imagined that finishing fourth from last would land me on the cover, a featured story that went to all 195,000 members.

If I had quit in the middle of the race, no one would have known anything about me, what I've been through, much less what I went through that day. As a result of the story, I have been approached by countless people battling their own demons and thanking me for the encouragement.

The article also had cosmic timing, coming out during the Kona Inspired Contest voting period—it required a nationwide vote to get me into the IRONMAN World Championships in Hawaii. The extra exposure went a long way toward helping my cause. You'll be amazed what you can accomplish in life if you'll commit to run one more mile or make one more sales call or ask one more girl out for a date. Worked miracles for me.

CHAPTER 5

Pain, Love, and Other Adventures

Anything worth doing, is worth overdoing.
—Mick Jagger

Pain and anger are something we all feel. Experiencing those emotions doesn't make us bad or weak people. The key is what we do with those emotions. It's natural to be angry when someone causes us pain, especially the kind that forever changes our life. But eventually you come to the realization being angry doesn't take away the pain and only slows the healing process. After years of trying to figure out what happiness was and more importantly what it wasn't, I finally convinced myself to choose happiness.

Happiness is a choice. Who doesn't want to be happy? No one can make me (or you) happy. It has to come from within. You have to convince yourself you are worthy of being happy and you deserve to be happy. Why should I let three minutes of one day as an eight-year-old determine how I feel the rest of my life? Trust me, it wasn't that I didn't experience feelings of depression and isolation, but I consciously decided to focus more on what was good in my life than what was bad. I had really seen the worst of the worst at the Shriners, and in comparison, my life was pretty awesome. When you put your tragedy in perspective with the struggles of others, it's a paradigm shift. There was nothing in life I couldn't do if I really wanted it bad enough. The key was how hard was I willing to work and what was I willing to sacrifice to make it happen.

Why do we choose to focus on the four or five bad things in our life and let those things alter our daily walk as opposed to focusing on the 15 amazing things in our life? When something unexpected and great happens in your life, do you stop and say "God, why me? I don't deserve this." Inversely, when something tragic happens do you stop and say "God, why me? I don't deserve this." If you're going to question the bad things in your life, you better question all the good too. When I look at all the blessings in my life, how could I not feel happy?

To be truly happy and move beyond unwanted feelings of doubt, anger and regret, I learned not to focus on what I've lost in life but rather to focus on what I've gained. I lost the innocence of my childhood. I lost my right ear and 65 percent of my body to severe scars. I lost the ability to feel adored and desired by girls. But look at what I gained as a result. I have an amazing and beautiful wife of 15 years who loves me unconditionally, scars and all. I have five healthy and uniquely gifted kids who know their daddy is the only dad who can take his ear on and off—their friends love it. I have a job where I get paid to talk about myself and share stories. I have competed in 10 triathlon World Championships across four continents. Tell me how I've missed out.

Grow or Die

It hasn't always been easy. Embracing my new reality was a process that evolved over years if not decades. Before the burn, I was an attractive, popular, and gregarious kid. Forming friendships was easy and natural. But after the accident, everything was suddenly different. No one looked at me the same. I was not the same eight-year-old boy … weak and fragile at first, but ultimately stronger and self assured. When it came to girls, I was insecure and lacked the machismo of my school mates. They all referred to me as their friend when I so desperately just wanted one of them to think of me as something more. I saw how they looked at the other boys and it was obvious they didn't see me the same way. Let's be honest, I didn't look anything like the other boys. None of them were missing an ear or had scars all over their body. I couldn't help but feel like a circus freak. Changing in the locker room for PE didn't help either. When I had my shirt off, I could feel eyes on me and every now and then I'd catch someone in a fixed gaze. My scars took on a completely different meaning without clothes.

As I got older, I embraced my situation, but more out of necessity than anything. I had to reinvent myself into something new. Something immune to stares, comments, and outright cruelty. I had to be a rock and I vowed to never let anyone or anything break me. Part of my hardening required internalizing the hurt and only showing tears of joy and happiness. No one knew of the pain I masked daily. It was bad enough I looked physically fragile, I definitely didn't want to bring more attention to myself by complaining and being perceived as emotionally fragile. I realized being the burn kid was not the life I wanted. I wanted more. I realized people were always going to make fun of me, so I might as well beat them to the punch. I also found it beneficial to be self-deprecating. Oddly, I didn't have an ear until I was 34 years old. In the eighties and nineties, the technology for a prosthetic ear was horrendous so I chose not to have one, hoping they'd have a better option at some point, not realizing it would be 26 years before that option would arrive.

Without an ear, I simply felt inadequate and unbalanced. For the longest time, I even grew Farrah Fawcett wings in my hair to cover up my ears—luckily, I parted with the wings in high school after a female barber asked if I wanted a "cool dude haircut." By the time I got to grad school, I had accepted I'd be a bachelor the rest of my days—but it wasn't from lack of effort.

Then I met Brooke.

Brooke worked at the UT student gym I frequented every day during graduate school. She was friendly, but definitely not interested in the "gun show" I showcased in the gym while hammering out curls. She was obviously out of my league but pursuing the impossible has always interested me.

Luckily, I had an in: one of my fraternity brothers, Kevin Parker, had been best friends with Brooke since high school. One night we had a few beers, and after midnight we got the idea of calling her. So, we did, and she made the mistake of answering. It went pretty well, considering, and the next day I got her number from Kevin with the caveat I'd not embarrass him. I called her, this time without the aid of liquid courage, and again, it went well. Seizing the opportunity and her moment of weakness, I invited her over for a cookout at my house, said "See you at six," and promptly hung up to eliminate the chance of her saying no. Conflicted, Brooke showed up and actually had a good enough time to agree to a real date. Truth be known, she agreed to a second date because she really liked my dog and figured I had to be a decent guy.

Doomed to Bad Luck
From Day One

Remember the 1 percent rule.

Date night arrived. On our way to a casual dinner at a local eatery called Darryl's, we were rear-ended while merging on the expressway. The car in front of us came to a complete stop, causing me to hit my brakes. Meanwhile, the guy behind me slammed into the back of my Bronco at 40 miles an hour, blowing out my back windshield and totaling his pickup truck. We were going to miss our reservations and I was furious, not because of the damage, but because we'd miss our reservation ... it's not like I have dates every week. After pleading with the police officer to be sympathetic to my situation, he let us go and we hurried to the restaurant. The kitchen was closed, but we managed to split a dessert and talk for a little while. I felt like I salvaged the night, unaware I was driving us around with a leaking gas tank—or that Brooke was suffering from whiplash.

Despite all that, she agreed to go out with me again, and I believe God sealed our fate right there: we've been overcoming obstacles together ever since—from the complications with each of her five pregnancies to her constant "I told you so" moments. I always kid with her that she knew what she was signing up for from day one, so she can't claim she wasn't warned. (More on this later.)

Loving Me Ain't Easy

Four months after Brooke and I began dating, I needed another major surgery. The scar band on my neck had become atrocious, pulling down the entire right side of my face. I was also losing my hearing. The plan was to seek treatment at a nationally recognized hospital with a reputation for treating burn patients, now that I had aged out of the Shriners program. The surgeon recommended doing a large skin graft to my neck and removing the previous graft to avoid a patchwork look. I took Brooke to the consultation so she could get an idea of the kind of things I go through, hoping she could understand why this stuff was hard for me to talk about. I wanted her to experience it without me having to tell her about it.

During the consultation, I told the surgeon I preferred having skin removed from my legs; he confirmed it wouldn't be a problem. The Shriners had used reharvested skin for my last skin graft and it produced amazing results. The surgery was scheduled for Valentine's Day of all days, and I'd planned to take only a week off school as I was preparing to graduate from the MBA program in the spring.

Remember the 1 percent rule.

Immediately after the surgery finished, the doctor walked into the waiting room and told my mom, "Everything went great. We decided to cut the front and back of his armpit and insert a skin graft from his back. We also took a nice graft from his right buttocks, and replaced the existing graft in his neck."

My mom knew this wasn't the surgery I agreed to and asked the doctor, "Shay was okay with this?" The doctor said, "Trust me, this is what was needed. We're confident he'll be happy with this."

In the recovery room, I woke up in immense pain. My back was extremely tender and my butt was killing me. *Something is sticking in me. Why am I hurting here?* The nurse told me I was going to be really sensitive to movement; the dressing over the donor site on my back was stapled in me. I said, "What ... my back? What do you mean stapled in me?" The doctor took skin off of my back the size of a piece of notebook paper and stapled it into my armpit. The dressing was physically stapled into my skin. When I moved, I could feel the staples ripping holes in my back.

As for the pain in my butt, they'd taken a skin graft off of my right butt cheek and stapled it into my neck. The dressing was physically stapled into my butt, one in my actual crack of all places. Also, not part of the plan.

I was in tears. I just couldn't believe it. *Are you kidding me? These had been the only two spots on my whole body with no scars whatsoever.* I'd intentionally preserved them my whole life for when I'd find THE life-changing surgery. Here's virgin skin that's untouched, the only part of my body with no scars, now permanently ruined. Not to mention half of my back is now permanently discolored and extremely sensitive to sun.

A plastic surgeon had mentioned once before they might be able to take skin from my buttocks to fix my face—its skin thickness closely matches your face. Now that was no longer an option.

Mom came into the recovery room in tears, too. We asked to speak to the doctor, but he was already out of town on a fishing trip for five days. When he called the next day, he explained the "little change in plans," that once I was on the operating table, he felt this was the best option for me. I don't doubt they did what they felt was best for me, but at the end of the day, this is my body. I told him, "You should have given me that option. I would have said no. That's the whole reason why we did a consultation, to talk through all of this." He replied, "Well I'm sorry that you feel that way, but I think over time, you'll come to feel differently."

Hell and Healing

Trying to return back to school in a week was a nightmare. The attending doctors recommended I take several weeks off to recover but I couldn't take off the necessary time if I was going to graduate on schedule. Equally important, I was also only one month into a new internship, working with renowned investor/entrepreneur Mike Crabtree, a distinguished alumnus of UT. Securing an internship with Mike was a dream come true and no way I was going to mess it up. It was my one shot to make my impact in the business world. The last thing I wanted was to let Mike down and fall behind on my work. I fulfilled my obligations during my hospitalization, emailing and compiling spreadsheets during dressing changes at my own direction. Another intern had started the same day as I did, and I wanted to demonstrate *I WAS THEIR GUY*. Surprisingly, the other intern was let go while I was out. Mike would also play a pivotal role in my life 18 years later.

When the skin was harvested from my back and buttocks, they put a dressing on it to help it heal. Healing required the donor site to scab over, but every time I sat down, it would rip open. I was bleeding through my pants, through my shirt, and—after an hour and a half of sitting in a class— I'd go to get up, only to find I was stuck to the chair; the scabs had dried, only to rip again when I stood up. I could feel blood dripping down my back and down my legs.

And this was my daily routine at school every day, constantly ripping and bleeding. It took three weeks for all this to heal. Brooke would come over twice a day to help me change the dressings I couldn't reach. It's pretty humbling and embarrassing having to get your girlfriend to change the dressing on your rear-end. (Luckily, she always thought my butt was one of my best assets.)

I tried using the UT's student escort service to get to and from class, but it wasn't reliable, so I decided to ride my motorcycle instead, due to favorable parking. I also managed to satisfy the commitment of my internship where I was working 30 hours a week. How I managed to fulfill all my obligations was nothing short of a miracle.

After the surgery, I was angry and internalized the hurt. It may be hard to believe, but I was angrier at the surgeon than at Becky for setting me on fire. Becky's mistake was purely an accident. The surgeon's mistake was pure arrogance. He was simply too busy to consider the impact of his actions. I went into it with high hopes this premier institution was going to fix my issues. I truly believed I was entering the surgery as the ugly duckling and would wake up as a beautiful swan. To say I had high hopes

> " I pushed her away, and we stayed split up for a year. We still talked and saw each other from a distance, but I had to heal from the inside out.

was an understatement. I felt I'd came out worse than when I went in. This was not the first time a surgery didn't go as planned, but it was the first time the surgeon changed the surgery while I was asleep. I'm not very good at talking about pain and even worse about expressing my emotions and disappointments. Brooke wanted desperately to help and hoped I'd let her in. The more she wanted to help the more I shut her out. I couldn't let her—it's just not me and it goes against my belief of complaining. Complaining never solves anything and I've always believed it was a sign of weakness. This was my cross to bear. Burying the emotional pain is all I've done for my entire life. I know that didn't make it right but it had gotten me through all the hard times as a kid. It was all I knew. I've never met with a therapist, never shared with anyone, never let anyone in. I pushed her away, and we stayed split up for a year. We still talked and saw each other from a distance, but I had to heal from the inside out.

I signed up for rugby during those months of separation—I'd never played in my life, but it was a way for me to deal with the anger I was feeling. Back-to-back weekend trips to the ER to get stitches to my right eyebrow let me know that maybe it was time to find another outlet, but the pain helped with the healing.

It's still hard for Brooke today to fully understand why I internalize my suffering. She accepts she's not going to change me, but that doesn't make it easier on her. I've always felt this is my burden, and the last thing I want to do is impose on others and make them feel sorry for me. I know I'm not battling alone, and I'm eternally grateful for that.

EAR DIARIES PART V:
SAND SHARK

My scars and my lack of a right ear are an attention-getter at the beach. In my senior year of college, I was at the beach building a sand castle when a young boy sidled up to me, offering to help. His mother stood within earshot distance a few feet away. Without missing a beat, the kid said, "Hey, where's your ear? And what happened to your arm?"—referring to the waffle texture of my skin grafts and the big depression in my arm from the last skin graft.

Never one to miss a golden opportunity, I told the kid, "Well, it may be hard to believe, but a few days ago I was wading out in the ocean, about waist deep, looking for sand dollars. I reached down to grab one and a sand shark latched onto my arm and the right side of my face. I started screaming and, luckily, my dad was able to grab me and keep the shark from dragging me out to sea. It was a close call, but thankfully he only got my ear and a big chunk out of my arm."

Dumbfounded and in complete shock, the mother quickly grabbed her son by the arm and said "Kyle, your dad is motioning for us." Then to me, "Thank you, sir, and glad you're healing nicely." I wondered if the kid went back in the ocean during his trip.

IRONMAN St. George

St. George, Utah

I'd just finished second in my age group in the Beach 2 Battleship Iron Distance race in November, prompting me to sign up for IRONMAN St. George, believing I could qualify for Kona. At the time that I registered for IRONMAN St. George, it was promoted as the hardest IRONMAN course on the circuit—and to me, racing 140.6 miles in the Mojave Desert sounded awesome.

I figured only fools would sign up for this race—perfect for me, right? Still relatively new to the sport (only my third season), I wanted to race the hardest courses.

Brooke and I arrived in Utah that May to find that it was 90 degrees. An unseasonably warm front moved in, creating some nice thunderstorms as well. Historically, at this time of year, it's 75 degrees.

Remember how I have trouble regulating my body temperature in hot weather? I had intentionally conditioned my training to match expected race conditions of 75 degrees. We arrived four days before the race to help acclimate to the altitude. Almost immediately, partially compounded by the barometric pressure change from the thunderstorms, I began getting migraines every day leading up to the race. Luckily, I had my migraine meds, but they took a lot out of me, and I was having to take them daily, including the night before the race.

The migraine eventually passed, but not till 2:00 a.m. I was wide awake and definitely not going back to sleep. But there was nothing to do but lie there until 4:00 a.m., when I would normally get up for the race. Migraine-free, my mind now started to contemplate the impact of both 90-degree race conditions as well as the lack of sleep on my abilities to qualify for Kona.

I had a pretty good 2.4 mile swim, but five miles into the bike ride, my chain dropped and sucked to the frame. I pulled over, spent five minutes getting the chain back on, and noticed my hands were covered in grease. I kept telling myself, *Hey, don't worry about it. It's a long day. You've got at least another nine hours out here. Don't panic; race your race.*

Back on the bike, I went hard; I had five bottles of specially for-mulated EFS nutrition on my bike and started reeling in other racers. Nutrition is absolutely critical to a successful race in IRONMAN. Everything felt great as I bombed down a hill at mile 10, hitting speeds of 50 miles per hour, absorbing the bumps of the rough chip tar surface, screaming with excitement—at least until two of the bottles sailed off the back of my bike. I glanced quickly to observe both bottles explode as soon as they hit the ground—a devastating occurrence, since each water bottle contained 1,866 electrolytes. I kept pushing the pace, keenly aware I'd inevitably be at a major nutrition deficit with 20 percent of my nutrition intake gone and more than 14,000 feet of elevation gain on the bike course to go.

With the 112-mile bike ride behind me, I noticed I was about 40 minutes off where I should be to be competitive. I was in pain and realized the heat, altitude, and electrolyte deficit were taking its toll. I needed to go to the restroom; I was extremely uncomfortable and I started peeing blood. I didn't panic but this was a first. I was extremely dehydrated; the impact was putting stress on my kidneys.

I was about to run a marathon on the world's hardest IRONMAN course through the Mojave desert with over 3,600 feet of elevation gain and I was peeing blood. I blocked out the pain, but my skin felt like it was on fire. Everything in me said *Quit. I'm hurting. I'm miserably hot. I'm not going to get my desired race time.* Yet as soon as I come out of the porta-potty to start the run, I saw Brooke and my dad. She said, "Hurry up, you gotta catch them!" I didn't dare tell her what was going on; I just gave her a kiss and said, "All right, babe, love you." And I took off running. There was no way I was going to quit after she'd stood in the hot sun cheering me on for over seven hours. I told myself *they'll have to drag me off the course before I quit.*

I was able to tap into reserves of will power and push through. I saw so many people walking and thought, *That's not going to be me. Just push through the pain, just run one more mile. You've been through worse.* I also drew strength from the two Navy Seals out there. I thanked them for their service, and all I could think was, *Man, if these guys are out here doing this in light of everything else they're doing, the least I could do is to suck it up and get through this.*

Somehow, I managed to push through the pain and cross the finish line in 11 hours and 13 minutes.

I finished in the top 20 percent, and medics immediately gave me an IV for my dehydration. I didn't win anything and I missed my chance of going to Kona, but I finished the job at hand and knew I truly gave it everything I had. What more could I ask of myself? Not every race can be a perfect race. When things go wrong, you reset expectations and push ahead.

CHAPTER 6

Making Lemonade Out of Lemons

> *You don't learn to walk by following rules.*
> *You learn by doing, and by falling over.*
> —*Richard Branson*

I f it weren't for a chance meeting with a man named Henry Forrest, I would never have competed in an IRONMAN, much less the IRONMAN World Championship in Kona.

I met Henry while working in Colony Square's high-rise office towers in downtown Atlanta. Every day at lunch, I'd go down and work out, focusing on what I thought everyone cared about: biceps and chest. It's how good you look in a T-shirt, right? I'll never forget the day I was changing clothes in the locker room when this sixty-five-year-old man approached me. Barrel-chested, with a crew cut, Henry came from a different cut—there was just something about him. He definitely didn't look like someone in the financial-services business.

He made a comment to me, "Hey, tough guy," and invited me to his daily boot-camp class. He said it was just him and a bunch of women doing stuff you learned in grade school: pushups, sit-ups, jumping jacks, squat thrusts. "Shouldn't be anything for a guy like you with all your muscles," he teased. I should've seen it coming: he was setting me up. I said, "Whatever, old timer. Sure."

Sure enough, it was me and maybe one other guy in the class, and all the rest were women. I proceed to get bested by them all. Henry dropped down beside me and hammered out four-count push-ups and yelled, "Eskew, you better pick it up. Ponytails is kicking your butt." Embarrassed, yet resolved to redeem myself, I returned to class the next day and every day thereafter. Within three months, I was back into what I call fighting shape. I'd lost 20 pounds, was feeling rock solid, and could actually keep up.

I found out that Henry was one of the original IRONMAN finishers from 1978. He was also a Marine drill sergeant, man of God, and a hugely inspirational man.

During those next few months, he was diagnosed with stage-four pancreatic cancer. I'll never forget, he was telling all of us what he was going through, the chemo, and as soon as someone would start to tear up, he'd say, "Get your feet moving. Don't you feel sorry for me. Not one tear, you hear me? Hit it." He was a man's man. He was doing chemo in the evenings and boot-camp classes at 6:30 a.m.

He and I began to talk about the uncertainties of life—that it doesn't matter how good a life you live; bad things happen to good people. He didn't drink or smoke. He'd been married to one woman and was faithful to her. He served his country, lived a good life. "I did everything the Good Book told me to do, but yet I still got cancer," he'd say. I told him I was just a kid minding my own business, next thing I know I'm on fire. We bonded, talking about how you make the most of the cards you're dealt.

> **"I did everything the Good Book told me to do, but yet I still got cancer," he'd say. I told him I was just a kid minding my own business, next thing I know I'm on fire.**

We lost Henry on November 8, 2008, and right before he passed away a group of us told him we'd do the next big triathlon in his honor. We didn't care about the distance.

Team Henry

It just so happened the next big triathlon coming up was a half IRONMAN in Panama City, Florida in May of 2009—the Gulf Coast Half IRONMAN. It was my very first triathlon: a 1.2-mile ocean swim with three-foot swells to start off—I'd never swum in open water. I didn't even own a bike when I registered. I bought a fluorescent green Cannondale road bike off Craigslist for $500. And I was not running at all—hated it, in fact.

But we did it, parading our "Team Henry" shirts around with immense pride. A few days later, my buddy and godfather to middle son Asher, Mike Miller, suggested we do IRONMAN Florida. Same course, but twice the distance. I was in. I even signed up that night; with just six months to prepare for a full IRONMAN, I was the only one to take the bait. No sane person does an IRONMAN their first season as triathlete ... but you obviously don't know me.

It also happened—unbeknownst to me—the one-year anniversary of Henry's passing fell on the day of IRONMAN Florida. The day before the race, his daughter spotted me in a crowd and told me, "Daddy will be cheering you on from heaven." I really think that's what got me through the race: knowing Henry was watching me. I wrote Henry's name on my right hand and that of my deceased father-in-law, Bill Etherton, who we'd lost to colon cancer in 2005, on my left to remind me during the race, *this is why you're doing it; it's bigger than you.*

All in the Family

Every obstacle in life is a learning and growth opportunity, including going into business with family when that's never what I envisioned for myself. After completing my MBA, I, reluctantly, and after some coaxing from my mother, decided to help my dad buy a 45-year-old automotive business. On July 3, 2001 we were the new owners of Brake Specialty Co. I agreed to put up the down payment, selling my stock and all I owned, and committing three years to make a run of it. Dad had sacrificed so much for me—it was the least I could do to help him pursue his dream. If we couldn't make it work in three years, I'd have to walk away.

Two months after acquiring the business 9/11 happened— nearly destroying our business. More than half of our income was tied to the airline industry, with Delta and AirTran being major customers. To avoid laying off any employees, and to offset the loss of income, I had to forgo a paycheck for six months and take a night job at Home Depot, working in hardware. I'll never forget the store manager asking during the interview "You have an MBA and you're willing to take this job for $11/hour?" I said "Honestly, my landlord doesn't care about my degrees, he just wants the rent. And, I'll take the job for $12/hour, not $11." Six months later our business recovered, and I was able to retire my orange apron. To add insult to injury, the following year our landlord raised the company rent 20 percent, forcing us to downsize and relocate our business. Despite the struggles, we doubled revenue by the end of year one and tripled revenue by the end of year two.

Five years later, October 2007, with only ninety days notice, we were forced to move yet again. We were in the new building less than 10 weeks when a tornado came through downtown Atlanta. On March 14, 2008, the tornado ripped the roof off the building we'd just vacated. Had we stayed there, it would have put us out of business completely. There was no way we could have recovered from our entire building and all our inventory and computers being saturated with water. Moving saved our business, and it just underscores the silver lining in everything.

We eventually sold the business on September 12, 2008, and just two weeks later the stock market crashed. The buyer wanted to delay the sale, but I refused. Had I agreed to their terms, we'd have received half the purchase price or gone out of business. It's no coincidence we bought BSC two months before the biggest terrorism act on US soil only to sell BSC two weeks before the biggest recession since the Great Depression. I wouldn't trade the experience of working side by side with my dad for the world. Regardless of the outcome, we went for it. We didn't play it safe and stand on the sidelines and say, *I wonder ...* We pursued dad's dream and gave it everything we had.

What we accomplished together was nothing short of a miracle. One of the greatest feelings in life is relentlessly pursuing your dreams, even if you come up short. No regrets.

When Opportunity Knocks

With the pending sale of BSC in September and two kids under three at home, I was in search of a new career. Unsolicited, a former business colleague suggested I meet her friend, owner of a property-and-casualty insurance agency. I didn't see myself as an insurance salesman, but I've always been open to meeting successful people. After all, I'd be out of a job soon, after the sale of BSC. During my first meeting with the man who would be my future employer, after being questioned if I could be successful in a sales producer role, I bet him my first two paychecks that he and I could do 10 cold calls together, but everyone would only remember me. Let's not forget I was 33 with no formal sales experience applying for a 100 percent sales role.

He looked at me with this little grin on his face—you've got to keep in mind, he was in his mid-to-late fifties, balding, sharply dressed, and very successful. He said, "All right, spill the beans, you've got my attention." I said, "Would you agree, statistically, that tall men and attractive women do well in sales?" He goes, "Yes, I think we all know that's true." I said, "Is it because they're tall and attractive or because those are attributes that make them memorable?" He replied, "Well, I'd definitely say that makes them memorable." I said, "No offense, but there are a lot of mid-50-year-old balding guys out there making sales calls every day, but there's only one one-eared burn guy, and that's me. Therefore, they will remember me over you every time."

He said, "All right, do you want the job or not?" I took it.

I got my prosthetic ear, after seemingly endless insurance-related hurdles, but not before I took advantage of the fact that my scars were an advantage, not a detriment. They made me memorable. It's not about how you look, it's how comfortable you are in the skin God gave you.

Ear It Comes

Remember the 1 percent rule.

Life is constantly trying to drag you down just when you think you've scaled the mountain. This is a fact I am keenly aware of. I spent almost a year getting my prosthetic ear approved as a "medical necessity" and "in network" and endured the excruciating process to make it happen. I even spent the previous year traveling the country interviewing top surgeons to find the perfect solution, including a meeting with a retired CIA disguise specialist I saw on Oprah.

I'll never forget Dr. Koenig of BlueCross BlueShield of Georgia personally calling to tell me he had approved my ear. He was moved by my story and I was beyond the moon happy I'd once again have a right ear. I couldn't believe it; I was in tears—don't worry, no one could see me. The approval included all the required surgeries to be performed by maxillofacial surgeon, Dr. Glenn Maron, team surgeon for Atlanta Braves. The first surgery involved drilling three screws (dental implants) into my skull where my new ear would be. The screws would stay under my scalp for three months to allow implant ossification (permanently bond) with my skull. The second surgery involved cutting holes through my scalp for the screws to penetrate and attach abutments. The abutments were connected via a titanium bar the prosthetic ear would snap onto. After the second surgery healed, another doctor, actually a dentist (Dr. James Davis), casted an ear out of clay, which later would be made of silicone and hand-painted by Dr. Davis to match—an unbelievable process. After fitting me with the new ear, Dr. Davis told me "stop by your barber and get him to line up your sideburns, no more excuses for them being different lengths."

The day before the surgery, because there's obviously no going back once the screws are drilled into my skull, I called our HR director to verify no change in coverage had been made since our company's health insurance had renewed on the first of the month, which was three days prior. Confirmed, no changes, surgery still covered under my insurance. Surgery went great and as planned.

Five days later I received a letter from a different insurance company notifying me the surgery wasn't preauthorized and I was responsible for the full amount of the charges. I called immediately to ask about the letter and learned a change had been made to the company's health insurance after the renewal date, but coverage was backdated to the effective date, which was the first of the month—three days before my surgery. Just to clarify, I had BCBS coverage the day of surgery, I had BCBS coverage when I left the hospital—and five days later a decision was made to switch to another company, and all benefits were made retroactive. You can't make this up. In the end, I had to engage an attorney to draft several letters over three months to finally get the surgery approved—but not before having to pay a new deductible and $1,500 in legal expenses.

In the end, however, it all worked out and I am grateful I was able to finally feel somewhat whole again. Many back down from big insurance companies ... but they obviously didn't know who they were messing with.

EAR DIARIES PART VI:
PILLOW TALK

I feel hotel staffs are in need of entertainment, and it's my job to provide some. One of my favorite ear jokes is to leave it on my pillow, giving the hotel cleaning staff a bit of a fright. Every time I do that, you can bet that when I return, my bed is never made up. I can just imagine them calling downstairs, "Uh, I don't know what to do. I think somebody might have been hurt?" I've also left it on the phone between the two beds with a little note that says, "Please be quiet, I'm on a conference call." Just recently, I checked out of a hotel to catch an early flight and realized I left something. I approached the front desk clerk and said "Sorry to bother you, but can I get my room key back? I left my ear on the nightstand."

PART III

I AM IRONMAN

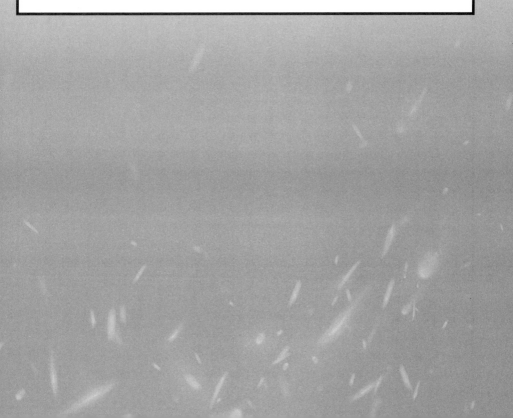

IRONMAN 70.3 World Championships

Zell am See, Austria

Earning a slot to compete in Zell am See had been the sole focus of all my efforts since September of the previous year. When they announced Zell as the host city, Brooke said, "I want to go. Do whatever it takes to qualify." In all my years of racing, she had never been so excited about a race venue, and I knew there was no way I could let her down. I went home that night and wrote "Qualify for Austria" on my whiteboard in my pain cave, a.k.a. my home workout room. I saw this message every morning and every night for nine months, reminding me of the task at hand—failure to qualify was not an option.

If you want to do something extraordinary, you can't keep doing what you've always been doing. Seizing the moment, I sent an email to Joe Friel, a world-renowned endurance coach and author of the *The Triathlete's Training Bible.* Joe personally emailed to say he was no longer coaching individual athletes, but he had an amazing coach who was a former IRONMAN 70.3 World Champion and a perfect fit for me—so in came Adam Zucco.

I was in the best shape of my life thanks to Adam's coaching. I'd just come off not one, but two of my fastest IRONMAN 70.3 times, back-to-back fourth-place finishes—4 hours, 27 minutes and 46 seconds at IRONMAN Chattanooga 70.3 and one second faster six weeks later at IRONMAN Muncie 70.3. My finish at Chattanooga in May earned me a Zell slot.

I arrived in Zell am See to find it was the most amazing place I'd ever seen. Fellow racers kept saying, "It's like you're racing in a postcard." The water was the bluest blue, the grass was the greenest green. No matter which direction I turned, everything looked surreal.

Remember the 1 percent rule.

I'd done all the preparation and training for race-day conditions. Normally the temperature for this time of year in Zell am See, Austria is 75 degrees—it'd been 65 on race day the previous year. This year, they decided to do the event at noon instead of 7:00 a.m., which is the time for the 50 other races I'd competed in the past eight years. And instead of 75 degrees, it was 90 degrees: the hottest day of the year. This has been a constant theme in my racing career: unprecedented record temps in my big race moments. Always the 1 percenter, I am.

But as soon as the time change happens, even I, Mr. Prepared, start to have concerns. I had been doing all my training assuming temps would be close to 75 degrees, and I'd be done with the race by noon. Now with it being 20 percent hotter, I knew I was going to be in a major deficit and had no choice but to embrace the suck.

I also knew the five-hour race start delay would have an impact. I had a routine for race day—wake at 4:00 a.m., eat pancakes and drink coffee at 4:15 a.m., read for 20 minutes and head to set my bike up around 5:30 a.m. During this time, my daily rhythms did their job. If I were a greyhound, I'd be the ideal pick. I should mention that the hotel had a petting zoo on its premises. (Is this an Austria thing?) A petting zoo in and of itself sounded cool—until we realized it included a donkey that hee-hawed every morning at the crack of dawn, like clockwork. Sleeping in was not an option.

All things considered, though, I felt relaxed at race time. After a really good swim, we began the bike ride. As we climbed up the Austrian Alps, the sun beat down and I could feel myself overheating. I was taking in all the fluids I was supposed to take in, but by the time I finished the 56-mile bike ride, I could not sweat anymore. I've never not been able to sweat, especially in 90-degree weather. This time, though, despite my great physical exertion, I was not sweating. I jogged with my fellow racer/friend Lucas Murnaghan for a mile but couldn't hold the pace. I began to get delirious while running, to the point where I started stumbling a little bit, forced to adopt a run/walk pace. I managed to squeak out an 8:23 pace for the half marathon.

I dug deep and crossed the finish line in 5 hours and 12 minutes. The course was worthy of a world championship. I told Brooke in the finish chute to meet me at the medical tent because I knew I was severely dehydrated, but the line was too long. I decided to skip it, man up, and take care of myself back at the hotel—definitely not my smartest decision. I'd already promised Brooke a dinner date to celebrate, but as soon as we hit the hotel room I started vomiting, which lasted two hours. My old "friend" diarrhea set in, too, so it was a party.

Crossing the finish line at Kona on the 2012 NBC broadcast of the IRONMAN World Championship. Notice my friend Feeney in the green shirt in the background?

Boy, 8, saves friend and himself

By Clem Richardson
Staff Writer

In one day of his eight years, Shay Eshew displayed more resourcefulness and courage and suffered more pain than most people might in a lifetime.

He is credited with saving his own life and that of a 7-year-old friend last month after they were accidentally drenched with gasoline while playing in a friend's yard.

Although his pain at times has abated, it has not ended. Thursday it included an operation in which his right ear was removed. It was the third operation the DeKalb County youngster has undergone in the eight weeks since the accident.

Shay and his friend, Jeff Brown, now share a room in the burn unit of the Shriners Hospital for Crippled Children in Cincinnati, Ohio. They remain in critical but stable condition.

"They argue over the television and fuss with each other," said Rick Eshew, Shay's father. "But they're doing a lot better than they were before."

The youngsters were burned Aug. 4 in a neighbor's home in Decatur.

Jan Eshew, Shay's mother, said it was about 3:30 p.m. when she ushered the boys outside to play in the yard. Ten

HAD 3 OPERATIONS FOR BURNS
Shay Eshew, 8

See BURN, Page 5-B

Burn

Continued From 1-B

minutes later, a neighbor's child ran to her back door and said that Shay had been burned.

The Eshews said neighborhood children have told them that another youngster was using gasoline to burn a wasps' nest, and somehow the two boys were set afire.

Witnesses said Shay raced across the street to his own yard, where he threw himself in the dirt and rolled over, partially extinguishing the flames covering the upper part of his body.

"He said he remembered to roll over from television," Shay's father said. "I asked him why he didn't roll over right there, and he said the bees would have gotten him."

Shay then ran back across the street and turned on the neighbors' garden hose, which he used to douse both his and Jeff's flames, Mrs. Eshew said. She wrapped the two boys up in blankets until the paramedics arrived to take them to Grady Memorial Hospital.

Shay suffered second- and third-degree burns over 35 percent of his body, all above the waist and mostly on his right side. Jeff suffered burns over 65 percent of his body.

Atlanta Journal and Constitution article featuring my story.

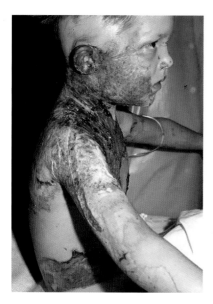 

This picture was taken when I was admitted to the Shriners. It's the last picture of me with a right ear. The large incision in my right arm was to relieve the swelling.

Christmas of 1983. Notice my right arm is stuck in a 45-degree angle. I also wore velcro shoes as I couldn't reach down to tie them.

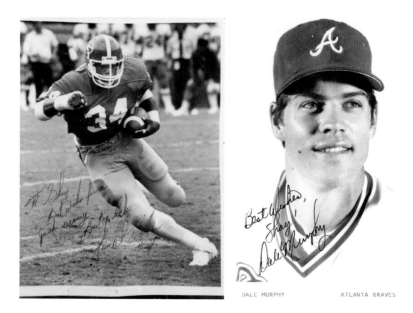

Autographed pictures of Hershel Walker and Dale Murphy I received in the hospital. Huge inspiration and reminder that others are silently cheering us on.

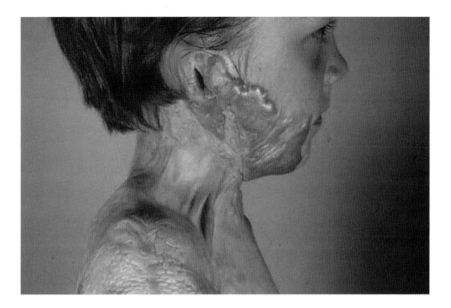

My burns 22 months after the accident. Notice the keloiding/thickening of the scar tissue. You can also see the scar bands on my neck that pulled my head to my shoulder.

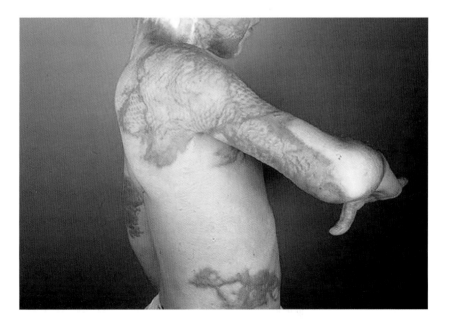

The waffle texture was a result of the machine used to stretch the grafted skin. Keloiding in full effect. It took almost eight years for the burn scars to turn from bright red to a normal skin color. I was not allowed to have sun on the burns for the first three years.

1980. Our last family photo before the burn. We definitely used our share of hair spray. I sadly adopted Mom's Farrah Fawcett wings after the burn.

1981. A lean, green hitting machine.

This is the last picture of me taken before the burn. So thankful my mom made all my clothes. I was sharply dressed, though!

Sixth grade, first year of wrestling.

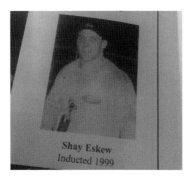

Inducted into the boxing hall of fame for my three-year, undefeated record.

Celebrating our 1991 wrestling team state championship victory. We won state all four years I was in high school. Individually, I finished forth in 1991 and state runner-up in 1992.

1999 championship fight. How were we in the same weight class?

The mama bear watching us from 30 yards away was not happy. The drug takes about 20 minutes to wear off and we have to stay with the bear until it does.

Always time for a selfie. I had already given him the drug to wake him up and had to make quick work of it.

Just hanging with the boys.

Bear wrestling. This guy was about 400 pounds.

My job was to be the distractor for this bear while the PhD student poked him in the hip.

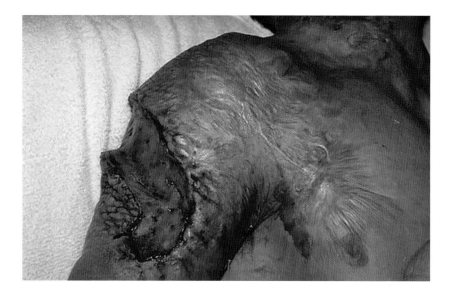

Here you can see what the divot looked like initially. My arm had become so tight over the years that it split open three inches when released—as shown. This is what my arm looked like for the next five years and gradually started filling in over the years.

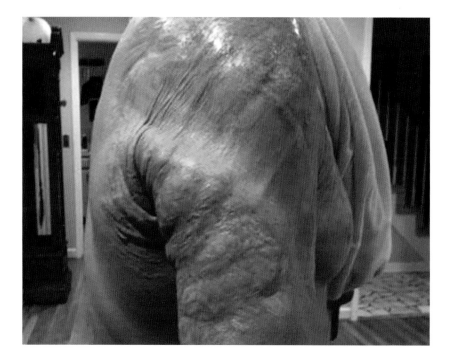

Fifteen years after they released the skin from my shoulder to the inside of my bicep.

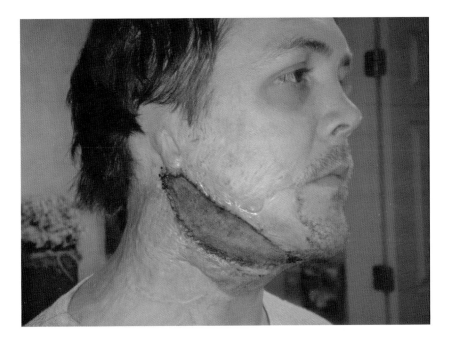

The tightness in my neck was so bad that it split open when released. The skin graft was harvested from my stomach—basically a tummy tuck.

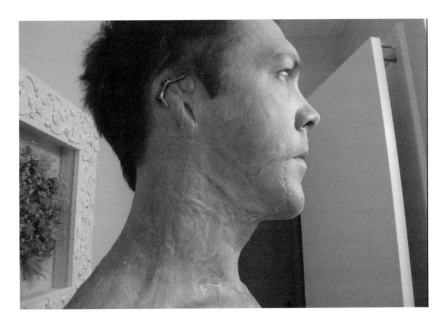

Fifteen years later, the skin graft looks great despite shrinking 55 percent. Here's a little secret: the big graft under this one came from my butt.

The totaled SUV with our luxurious Ryder truck in the background. Notice the hole in the windshield where the sign came through and just barely missed my head.

1999. Brooke and I when we first started dating. She didn't stand a chance.

Team Henry: all fellow boot campers who raced the Gulf Coast Half in Henry's honor.

Without Henry Forrest, one of the original 13 IRONMAN finishers, I'd have never gotten to IRONMAN.

2009 Gulf Coast Half, my first triathlon with Brooke, Nona, Aunt Vin, and Uncle Mike cheering me on.

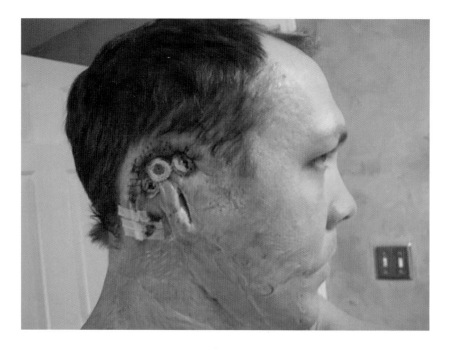

When the abutments were attached to the screws implanted in my head, they looked like bullets. You can only imagine the looks I received in public.

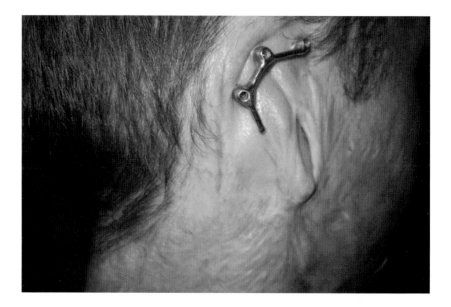

Final product of implants with metal bar attached. The prosthetic ear just snaps onto the bar. I get compliments about my "cool piercing" all the time.

Celebrating with my dad and sister Britney after crossing the IRONMAN Florida finish line.

2009 IRONMAN Florida bike leg.

2009 IRONMAN Florida Team SQ cheer section—Brooke, Marilyn, Joe Cat, Yogi, Aunt Vin, Uncle Mike, Olivia, and Maddox.

Me, Olivia, Maddox, and Asher running the annual Franklin Classic.

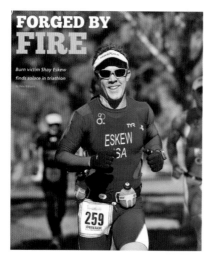

2011 ITU Long Course World Championships. My perseverance through two flat tires and running barefoot for six miles landed me on the cover of the *USA Triathlon* Olympic preview issue. Photo by Pete Williams.

2011 IRONMAN St. George. I had just peed blood and about to start the marathon. I crossed the finish line 3 hours 54 minutes later. Medical tent provided a quick fix.

Riding indoor on my bike trainer to train for Kona before I built my dream "pain cave." My pain cave at my mother-in-law's house was a small section wedged between kids toys and the cat litter box.

This is how much I consume during the bike portion of an IRONMAN race.

The pain cave is used by the entire family. We've now upgraded to include a Peloton for Brooke.

The day before Kona. Locked and ready.

Finally out of the water and ready for the 112-mile bike ride.

The marathon portion of Kona. I'm always conscious of photographers and smile despite what's really happening inside. Here I have my eye on the next porta potty.

My Kona dream complete. Final race time: 10 hours 45 minutes 49 seconds.

Team SQ cheer squad at Kona—my dad, Olivia, and Maddox.

Brooke and the kids drew this on the run section of Kona.

Me and Fireman Rob at
the Kona Parade of Nations

Sheryl Crow rallying her fans to compete
at Kona in the IRONMAN World Championships.

Photo by Rebecca McVay to help with the Kona Inspired voting.

Me and Chrissie Wellington at USAT Nationals. I'll never forget her encouragement at Kona; she's one of a kind.

Me and Dave Mirra at 2014 IRONMAN 70.3 World Championship. Dave "Miracle Boy" was a BMX iconic figure, X-Games legend, and super nice guy.

Me and Sister Madonna Buder, a.k.a. the Iron Nun, at USAT Nationals. My hero!

Me and Craig Alexander at the 2012 IRONMAN 70.3 World Championships. I wish I had worn my heels that day.

As you can see, Brooke was thrilled with me on our honeymoon. I failed to mention the bike ride down the volcano required catching a shuttle at 3:00 a.m.

Yes, Dad gave me permission to print this photo. Not only was it his worst nightmare, it will now be memorialized forever.

The kids wanted to visit Parrot Mountain near Dollywood.

The IRONMAN Foundation Newton Ambassador Triathlon Team with Wendy Lee of Newton Running and Dave Deschenes of IRONMAN Foundation. Love my Green Peeps!

Sharing my experience about the IRONMAN 70.3 Chattanooga course at the Team IMF breakfast.

IRONMAN Foundation (IMF) teammates Cynthia Steele, Ed Shifflett, and Darrell Freeman are all checked in for the IRONMAN 70.3 World Championship. Our service project provided children with swimming scholarships.

Just a pair of ears and shoes ... nothing to see here.

This is how hotel staff found my ear.

Accessorizing takes on a whole new meaning with multiple ears.

Got this one 50 percent off. What a bargain!

2018 family spring break trip to Yosemite. I forget to mention to Brooke we'd be hiking in snow, but I knew we wouldn't turn around and drive home once we got there.

From left to right: Olivia (12), Beckett (6), Maddox (10), Stella (4), Asher (8).

Shay Eskew

FUTURE ✓ +

Within twenty years from now I hopefully will have graduated from college with an architectural degree. I will pursue my architectural desire, by starting from the bottom with a small business firm, as I gain experience & I would move the ladder to where I eventually own my own company.

After about ten years of working I would have enough money to have a luxurious penthouse along with a slick convertible Mercedes. As time progressed it would get richer and be able to support my parents hopefully for the rest of their lives.

But most of all whether I am rich or not in the future I hopefully will be a successful Christian, which is more rewarding than any other riches on earth.

When I was 14, I wrote my vision for the future. It's refreshing to see as a kid I knew I would only get to the top by doing the hard work and working your way up—no free rides.

So how did I do?

- Graduate from college: MBA and BS, cum laude.
- Pursue architectural desire: changed majors 1.5 years into program.
- Own my own company: yes, sold it September 12, 2008, two weeks before the crash.
- Own a penthouse: I sleep on the top floor of my house, does that count?
- Own slick convertible Mercedes: Yes and no. I own a Mercedes, but a convertible is not practical with five kids.
- Support my parents: luckily they're both still in good health
- Be a successful Christian: Absolutely. I'm eternally grateful for the gifts I've been given and work hard to help others realize their potential.

CHAPTER 7
Road to Kona

*The human body was designed to work. The problem
is that little pea-sized brain gets in the way.*
—Henry Forrest

Over the years I've learned how to manage a busy training schedule with a busy household and career. How? I have to get the workout done in the morning, or it's not going to happen; I assured Brooke I wouldn't skip family time to train.

On an average day, I wake up at 4:00 a.m., walk the dog, have a cup of coffee, eat two blueberry waffles, and then I read business and inspiration books for 20 minutes. I can't emphasize enough the power of reading—helps set your whole day in the right frame of mind. Then I'll fire off work emails before starting my workout. I want my email to be the first email in everyone's email box when they arrive at the office. At 5:00 a.m., I start my workout, which is usually two hours long with a mix of biking, running, and/or swimming, each day predetermined based on what Coach Adam has planned.

To squeeze everything in, you have to be a little selfish with your time. So many people and circumstances, intentionally or unintentionally, steal your time. Time is your most valuable commodity, and it can't be replaced. You've got to learn how to say no to things that don't contribute to obtaining your goals or spending time with your family.

Longevity in IRONMAN is a lifestyle. Training is as much a daily routine as brushing your teeth; I just feel dirty without it. If we go on vacation, and we're driving there, I'll take my bike and my Wahoo trainer, which is what I put my bike on to ride indoors. I set them up inside the hotel or condo, allowing me to still train in the mornings while everyone's sleeping. It may sound drastic, but a commitment is commitment, rain or shine, vacation or no vacation.

When I began my IRONMAN training in 2009, then with only two kids under four, I showed Brooke the 30-week training plan taken straight from the book *Be Iron Fit* by Don Fink. He stressed, "Make sure you show your spouse what's involved. Ask them, 'What's important to you? What about this scares you? What trade-offs can I provide?'" Admittedly, it is a total family sacrifice. The term "Iron Widow" exists due to spouses becoming self-consumed in their quest and ignoring their family responsibilities. In support of me pursuing my dream, Brooke said, "I just need two days where I can sleep in and recover." Perfect. Every Sunday and Monday she gets breakfast in bed and I take the kids.

In peak mode, Saturdays are a big strain; a seven-hour workout consisting of a six-hour bike ride and one-hour run immediately after, with all training done by noon. I did my long run on Sunday right after church, which coincided with the kids' nap time. In all, I was logging 20 to 25 hours a week in training for IRONMAN. As we had kid number three and were planning on kid number four, I knew my days of racing IRONMAN were limited. It got to a point where I felt guilty, self-imposed mind you, leaving Saturday mornings at 5:00 a.m. only to come home six hours later and see the kids playing in the backyard with Brooke, knowing I still had another hour of training to go. To me, the physicality of training was easy, but the mental anguish of being away from the family was unbearable. I had to remind myself there was a bigger goal in mind and a certain date it would come to an end. In the summer of 2011, after my disaster at IRONMAN St. George, I told Brooke I was done racing full-distance IRONMAN and would only do small local events, convinced Kona just wasn't in the cards.

Kona Inspired ... Anything is Possible

When one door closes, another one opens. Early 2012, my friend Jennifer Porter found me at the Rev3 Knoxville race and made me aware IRONMAN was hosting a new contest for inspirational athletes. It was called Kona Inspired, a nationwide contest in search of six of the most inspiring stories, as determined by the voting public, to compete in Kona. Convinced it was a God thing and my dream within reach, I sat down with Brooke and asked, "Are you on board with me doing this? If I enter, I'm going to win. I know it." On July 20, I was picked as one of the six winners—but not before I got assistance from none other than the singer Sheryl Crow.

Nashville is a bubble. It's a place where stars are woven into everyday community life and no one bothers them. My son just happened to be on the same tee-ball team as Sheryl's son; it helped that my friend Taylor Irwin was the coach. We also had the son of Brad Paisley and Kim Williams-Paisley on the team. Come game day, they were just another parent on the sideline. ESPN College GameDay sportscaster Chris Fowler even showed up for one of our games.

Sheryl heard about the Kona Inspired contest from Taylor and sent me a text saying, "Shay, this is Sheryl Crow. I'm going to help you get to Kona. I'll have my social-media guy call you." Within two days, my Kona Inspired video appeared on her Facebook page with a message, "Please help my friend Shay Eskew get to Kona." Sheryl also got Brad, Kim, and Scott Hamilton to tweet "Vote for my friend, Shay." With my star-studded backing and God's will at work, I knew Kona was a lock.

Completely unsolicited, my high school friend, Chris Stalcup, employed with the largest marketing firm in the country, offered to bring his entire crew to town to create a powerful video, free of charge. (I can't even imagine what this cost!) They spent two days filming me swimming, biking, and running throughout the city (video can still be viewed on YouTube). When asked why he was doing this, he just said, "The world needs to hear your story." Two weeks later, I was swimming at the county community pool when I was approached by another individual who told me he'd like to help support my cause as well. He introduced himself as Thad Beaty, and upon inquiring about his professional vocation, he said he was in a band. "Oh really, I asked. Which one?" "Sugarland," he said. "Ah, yes I've heard of the band," I replied nonchalantly. Thad is Sugarland's guitarist. Thad is also an IRONMAN finisher with an amazing story. The support that flooded in from every direction was beyond belief.

It was also during the Kona Inspired voting period that USA Triathlon ran my cover story, "Forged by Fire," highlighting my 2011

ITU World's finish, completely unplanned and just another example of how Kona was a God thing. Unsolicited, I also received an invitation to share my story at Dave Ramsey's Devo event, a weekly inspiration session he holds for his employees. It was apparent to me I was meant to share with the world how God had used adversity to bring me the greatest blessings in my life: Brooke and my five amazing kids—Olivia, Maddox, Asher, Beckett, and Stella. Gaining entry into Kona was a major hurdle, but finding the money to travel there with my entire family (four kids under six at the time) was another. I couldn't imagine crossing the finish line at Kona without them there. To monetize my effort, I sold advertising on my race kit—including to a random stranger, Joel Shapiro, who I met in the line at Starbucks in Atlanta.

Rushing to get back home for my niece's bithday party, I popped into Starbucks for a jolt of energy. Standing in line, I noticed Joel was wearing a running outfit and Newton running shoes, the same ones I've raced in since 2009 and who has sponsored me as an Ambassador Athlete since 2011. I struck up a conversation about his Newtons. Turned out, he was an investor in Newton; he gave me

> **The outpour of support covered our travel expenses and allowed me to donate leftover funds to the Shriners.**

his card. After being notified I won a Kona Inspired spot, I emailed Joel about my Kona journey as well as my need to raise funds. He donated $10,000 to my cause and introduced me to former Navy Seal Todd Ehrlich, who provided his sports-recovery drink, KILL CLIFF, for all my Kona training. The outpour of support covered our travel expenses and allowed me to donate leftover funds to the Shriners.

Kona was truly a God thing. We never know how the people we interact with today may impact our lives a year or five or even 20 years later. What's even more amazing about Kona is if I had competed as a result of my own efforts, qualifying like the other athletes, no one would have known my story. But competing under God's plan allowed me to share my story with the world, hopefully motivating thousands. We are so quick to judge life under "our plan." I have learned that if I embrace the obstacles and have the patience for God's plan to be revealed, my life will be enriched beyond my wildest dreams.

But I wasn't the only winner. I also met some other incredibly inspiring individuals via the contest, including my friend Rob Verhelst, a.k.a "Fireman Rob." Rob wears a fireman's full gear for the marathon portion of the race. Another is Brady Murray, racing for his son to raise awareness for kids with Down's syndrome. I also had the honor of meeting Mike Thompson, who was diagnosed with leukemia at age 10 but refused to let it slow him down.

One remarkable thing I've learned through this experience is everyone has a story.

Transforming into IRONMAN

My whole life has been about constructing my mind and body into something I wanted. I learned early we're all capable of shaping our destiny. There's so much in life we have no control over and we can't lose sleep over those … but if we commit 110 percent effort to changing the things we can control, life takes on a new meaning. When I was eight, I willed myself into becoming a baseball player by adopting an unnatural throwing style. All through my high school career, I forged myself into a competitive wrestler through diet and relentless exercise. When I got into college, I constructed myself as a competitive boxer. I strengthened my mind by adopting a you'll-have-to-kill-me-to-beat-me attitude and chiseled my body by dropping 20 pounds to become capable of going three rounds all out, never giving my opponents a moment's rest. After college, I fashioned myself as a strong man and added 15 pounds of muscle mass, serving me well when performing feats of strength (squatting nearly 2.5 times my weight) on a mission trip in Morocco. Ten years post college, I undertook the ultimate transformation, that of becoming an IRONMAN. I dropped 40 pounds in total and relentlessly shaped my body into 146 pounds of lean muscle capable of competing 11 hours without stopping. Equally important, I hardened my soul to withstand whatever life can throw at me. I know no matter what challenges life presents, I am up for the challenge. I'll never quit.

I knew I had a major shortcoming going into the IRONMAN World Championships, because I couldn't sweat on one-third of my body and with the other two-thirds, I couldn't *stop* sweating. My body has no ability to thermoregulate and racing through a lava field all but guaranteed severe dehydration, if not hospitalization.

My whole life I'd thought I just couldn't handle the heat. And then a dietitian, Mari-Etta Parrish, reached out to me when I got into Kona. She'd heard about my story and knew I would need all the help I could get. Mari-Etta donated her expertise and detailed nutrition plans to see me achieve my dreams.

Call me neurotic, but I spent three months weighing myself five times a day. I'd weigh myself when I'd wake up, right before a workout, after a workout, mid-day, and before going to bed. I charted fluids consumed, heart rate, weight loss, and outside temperatures during workouts to calculate my sweat rate. To have any chance of being competitive at Kona, I needed to drink 1.5 liters per hour for 10 hours straight.

One day on a five-hour bike ride covering 110 miles, I averaged 21.2 miles an hour with an average heart rate of 131. During the ride, I drank 10, 24-ounce water bottles, which was almost two gallons. Before the workout, I weighed in at 146.2 pounds. After the workout, I was 143.4 pounds, and that's after drinking two gallons of fluid. I sweated out 20 pounds during the workout, keeping me right at the targeted 2 percent net body weight loss, and let's not forgot I'd still have to run a marathon through a lava field. It's hard to fathom drinking a bottle of water every 30 minutes for 10 hours straight. My ability to compensate for severe dehydration would determine whether I achieved my life dream or failed miserably.

Squeezing in training for IRONMAN required keeping workout gear with me at all times, even if it was only to get in a 20-minute workout. I utilized lunch breaks for my swim workouts.

I tracked my fluid output and heart rate (HR) every workout so I could calculate what was needed to be competitive at Kona.

Sample long bike ride (Saturday): 5 hours, 110 miles
Average MPH: 21.2
Average HR: 131 average HR
Consumed: 10 bottles (2 gallons), each bottle had 200 calories
Consumed: 450 calories/hour and 2000mg sodium (including liquid gel GU)
Weight Before: 146.2 lbs
Weight After: 143.4 lbs
Sweat rate: 19.5 lbs

Sample long run workout (Sunday): 30-minute bike ride then 3-hour run
Bike: 30 min, 10 miles, high RPM (target 100 RPM), 130 average HR
Run: 3 hours, 23.33 miles, HR range 147-152
Consumed: 6 bottles (1.2 gallons), each bottle had 100 calories
Weight Before: 146.4 lbs
Weight After: 142.4 lbs
Sweat rate: 14.5 lbs

Many a time, I've forgotten my towel and had to dry off with paper towels in the changing room. Other times, I've used my Hilton Honors status to use their gym on long layovers, stopping in for a quick run on the treadmill. In L.A., I rented a beach cruiser for a 20-mile ride. I'm a big believer doing something is better than doing nothing. Your heart doesn't know the difference. All it knows is how hard it has to work to get the body moving.

The last three weeks before Kona, I focused on heat acclimation, getting my body ready for the competition. I traveled to every work conference with my bike, my Wahoo bike trainer, and a heater. I heated up my hotel room to 100 degrees and would do a one-hour bike workout in the room twice a day, fully dressed in thermal underwear and a toboggan cap. Seeing me clad in cycling shorts at health care conferences is common. I never travel for work, or even vacation for that matter, without my workout gear.

> **I sweated out 20 pounds during the workout, keeping me right at the targeted 2 percent net body weight loss, and let's not forgot I'd still have to run a marathon through a lava field. It's hard to fathom drinking a bottle of water every 30 minutes for 10 hours straight.**

It sounds like a lot of hassle, but it's a commitment. A commitment to quit making excuses for not achieving your goals and saying *I'm too busy*. I will never fail to achieve my goals because I didn't prepare, mentally and physically. Besides, this was Kona, my dream, and I was *all* in. You only get one shot at your dream and I wanted the satisfaction of knowing, regardless of the outcome, I did everything I could to prepare myself.

If you approach everything in life with this all-or-nothing attitude, you'll be amazed at what can happen—and you'll never have any regrets.

EAR DIARIES PART VII:
ADULT SWIM

When I was 14, my friend Brian Fuchs and I were at his neighborhood pool. When I take my shirt off, it's very obvious I've been in a serious accident. On this particular day, I was in the deep end jumping off the diving board when these smaller children came up to me and asked, "Hey, where's your ear?"

I replied, "What do you mean?" I reached up and said, "Oh, crap. Where is my ear? I hit my head on the diving board a while ago trying to do a gainer. I must have knocked my ear off." All these kids ran around the deep end and were scanning the water. They yelled, "Hey, I see it. It's on the drain." (Which it wasn't—but for some reason, they're all convinced that it was.) I said, "Can you guys help me get it?" I knew they couldn't swim down deep enough to the drain. One by one they swam down three to four feet and came back up out of breath. "We can't get it." Then the lifeguard blew the whistle, and said, "Hey, it's adult swim. Everybody needs to get out of the water." These kids were panicking, "What are you gonna do about your ear?" I said, "I'll just get the pool skimmer net once the pool closes at the end of the shift."

IRONMAN
Edinburgh 70.3

Edinburgh, Scotland

What fun would an IRONMAN 70.3 race be if you didn't have drama? When I say drama, I mean that this race had drama of epic proportions, and all of my own doing. Remember the 1 percent. Embrace the suck!

Two weeks before IRONMAN Edinburgh 70.3, I surprised Brooke on her fortieth birthday with an adult getaway to Turks and Caicos with our favorite couple in Atlanta, the Pelletiers. We had an amazing trip, until I decided to sneak in a 10-mile run the morning of Father's Day while everyone was sleeping. Six miles into the run, I ran out of water and wasn't about to walk and short change myself. Improvising, I decided to refill my water bottles from a sprinkler system of a nice resort—yes, I'm painfully away how stupid this was.

I finished the run and felt great the remainder of the day and decided not to tell Brooke of my water issue. However, at dinner that night, Montezuma's revenge set in and I spent the majority of the night and wee hours of the morning in the bathroom. Brooke is well accustomed to my poor judgement and has adopted a "no sympathy" mentality—I'd expect nothing less. Upon arrival back in Nashville, I kissed the kids, distributed their souvenirs, exchanged my island bags for my work luggage, and caught a flight three hours later for our biggest work conference of the year.

Upon landing in Orlando, Florida for the conference, I didn't feel quite right, but there was no way I was missing the opening reception. I was sweating uncontrollably in my suit as I talked with prospective clients and praying they couldn't notice. At one point, I literally stopped mid-sentence and sprinted to the restroom and couldn't leave for 45 minutes. I suffered through the night and decided at noon the next day that enough was enough. A local urgent care clinic hooked me up with a heavy injection of Cipro.

At the conclusion of the conference, I flew home and 10 hours later was boarding yet another plane for Edinburgh, Scotland with my entire crew. Cipro did its job, but I also experienced one of its side effects—constipation. I couldn't use the bathroom for over seven days, definitely not what you want going into an IRONMAN 70.3 race on one of the world's hardest courses. Brooke told me it was insane to race when I could barely bend over to tie my shoes after consuming two boxes of stool softeners with no relief. I told Brooke there was no way I could back out. *If I can walk, I'm racing.*

Remember my race day ritual ... pancakes and coffee three hours before the race? Apparently, the Scots don't have Eggo frozen pancakes, just potato cakes. However, I did locate a McDonalds across the street from the race shuttle location and determined they were open 24 hours and had pancakes on the menu. Problem solved, except they didn't start serving pancakes until 5:00 a.m. and I was in the drive thru at 4:30 a.m. Realizing I couldn't race on an empty stomach, I opted for a double cheeseburger instead. Breakfast of champions, no doubt.

Race start conditions were the worst I had ever experienced, but the locals told me it was a traditional Scottish morning, cold, raining, and gusting winds. Twenty percent of the athletes registered didn't even start or failed to finish within the cutoff. The Firth of Forth was raging and could have easily been the setting for any Coast Guard rescue scene. The ocean swells created a nasty chop and crashed ferociously on swimmers trying to make their way out to the first turn buoy. Just waiting for the start was brutal ... the outside temperature was 50 degrees and the rain and wind cut right through you. I shivered uncontrollably standing in line to enter the water, constantly reminding myself *you got this*. Ultimately, conditions were so bad they cut the swim course in half due to dangerous rip tides, even for the pros. The water temperature was a crisp 54 degrees ... just another shock factor on top of the chaos playing out in the water.

I survived the swim, but there were touch and go moments. I jumped on the bike and was determined to start reeling in the other racers. As soon as I dropped down on my aero bars it became apparent that would not be the case. I was in excruciating pain. I tried to tough it out for the first 10 miles, but the constipation pains prevailed. I had to sit up for the remaining 46 miles and kept reminding myself *you're racing in Scotland through unbelievable landscape, celebrate the fact you're able do it*. I knew before the race started I wouldn't be in the top five, but I kept holding out hope maybe I'd get a bowel movement during the race and be set free. The ride was technical with a picturesque route snaking through the hills of the Lammermuirs. The race organizers even inserted a nice climb at the end over a dormant volcano (Arthur's Seat). This bike course was definitely one of the most challenging I had raced.

Three hours later, I dismounted the bike and started the 13.1 mile run through the beautiful Holyrood Park. I kept telling myself *the hard part is done. Now all you have to do is run a four-mile loop three times* (I never count the last mile, that's a gimme). No problem. Still wanting to get the full experience of pushing myself without doing irreversible damage, my goal was to run an eight-minute pace and not walk at any point. Even when you're not having a great race, you still need to set goals and reset expectations. I was still very uncomfortable, but being upright made all the difference in the world.

My mood was quickly lifted as soon as I saw Brooke and the kids standing on the side of the road. I feared the cold and the rain would deter them from braving the elements—not to mention keeping them entertained while waiting for the small two-minute window they'd catch a glimpse of me before I ran out of their sight. Perched up on the road side, I heard them yelling and I was able to high five all the kids and steal a kiss from Brooke before I started the three out-and-back runs to Arthur's Seat. As I ran, I decided to give every kid along the route a high five if their arms were outstretched. I truly believed each high five provided the additional power to push the pace. I felt I owed it to myself and especially to Brooke and the kids. I told myself over and over *you can embrace any amount of pain for six hours*. Luckily it only took 5 hours and 29 minutes, over one hour off my best time but still placing me in the top 20 percent. I was ready to celebrate but decided to skip the haggis! No sense pushing my luck.

CHAPTER 8
Kona at Last

> *You're not a great athlete, but you're*
> *one hell of a competitor.*
> *— Ace Miller[5]*

n the months building to Kona 2012, I was training on average
20 hours a week while working a full-time new job in a new
industry and raising a family. At peak training, I was up to
25 hours a week, and only taking Mondays off. Coworkers questioned my commitment to my job. They couldn't comprehend how
someone could get it all done. Luckily, I knew better than to listen
to naysayers. So many try to talk you out of audacious goals because
they are too scared to pursue their own. Prior to getting into Kona I

---

5   Ace Miller is the former national president of Golden Gloves. Coincidentally, he
     died on my birthday (March 8) in 2012.

had already completed three races that year; I finished seventh at the Rev3 Knoxville half-iron distance race, first overall in a local sprint triathlon, and second in another.

My quest to not only race Kona but be competitive meant competing at USAT Age-Group Sprint Nationals that August; the IRONMAN 70.3 World Championships three weeks later in September; and then, five weeks later, the IRONMAN World Championships. I also agreed to do the New York City Marathon three weeks after Kona on behalf of a charitable organization. It was a few pretty insane months.

Not only was I physically prepared, but I was mentally ready as well. I learned a lot that year, especially at the IRONMAN 70.3 World Championships in Las Vegas, Nevada, losing 6 percent of my body weight during the race as temps soared to 104. Although I knew better, I made the mistake of using course-provided nutrition instead of my proven EFS race mix, thinking I would be faster without the extra bottles hanging off the back of my bike seat. *IRONMAN Rule No. 1: never try something new on race day!* I finished 10 pounds under the weight I started with that day—139 pounds, the lightest I've been since age 18—sweating out a total of 25 pounds during the five-hour race. I had to do whatever it took to make sure I stayed on top of my nutrition—thank goodness Mari-Etta Parrish and her invaluable nutrition program rescued me.

With every race, there is a lesson. I have done a lot of learning since I started racing.

The IRONMAN Elite

While I was at Kona, I got the Kona Inspired VIP treatment, which entailed meeting some really inspirational people, like Julie Moss.

Julie is an IRONMAN icon and made IRONMAN famous in 1982 in the ABC televised broadcast of her collapsing within 200 feet of the finish line, completely unable to upright herself to secure her first-place finish. Julie exerted unfathomable courage and crawled on her elbows across the finish line to claim a heartbreaking second place, the winner having passed her during the crawl to the finish line. Julie had the finish line insight and then she collapsed in mid stride, her body shut down before your eyes. When folks watched her heroic finish, they thought to themselves, *I want a piece of that*. She is the reason so many people are in the sport today. Julie racing in 2012 marked the thirtieth anniversary of her initiation into IRONMAN. As luck had it, our bikes were racked next to each other in the bike transition and we were able to exchange pleasantries.

I also got to meet four-time IRONMAN World Champion Chrissie Wellington. She wasn't racing that year, but we spoke before the race started. She said, "Hey, good luck today." This phenomenally humble woman redefined how women compete in IRONMAN— oftentimes beating many of her male counterparts. She said, "Just stay calm. It's going to be a long day. The key is to keep yourself cool. At every aid station on the bike, grab a water bottle. Just pour it over your head " That's all I kept thinking about the whole race.

I also got to meet Sister Madonna Buder, also known as the Iron Nun. She's in the *Guinness Book of World Records* for the oldest IRONMAN finisher at 82. She entered the sport "as a way of tweaking mind, body, and spirit." She is an amazing woman, and I was privileged to meet her on a few occasions, but the first time was at Kona.

The Underpants Run

When I got into Kona I wanted to use the experience to impact the lives of others, and I thought, *Who better than my dad?* My dad is a salt of the earth man who is always too busy helping others to take care of himself. Like so many, he had gained unwanted weight over the years and unsuccessfully pledged to lose the weight only to become a victim to excuses.

Shortly after getting accepted into the race, I called Dad at work and informed him I had registered him for a weight-loss clinic. It was nonrefundable and I had prepaid for the class using his credit card. And if he was tempted to back out, he would have to call my sister and Mom and explain why he was quitting. *No more excuses … make it happen!*

By the time Kona came around, Dad had lost more than 40 pounds and was a new man. Upon showing up in Kona to cheer me on, he was convinced by yours truly to do the Underpants Run (a charity race where participants run in their underwear) with me. In support of my Kona effort, he signed up.

Brooke claims the image is still burned into her head (imagine taking a photo of your father-in-law in his tighty whities with your husband). As we were waiting for the run to start, Dad told me he was living his worst nightmare: being in public in his underwear.

Dad's support of me is something special, and I hope I can do the same for my kids. He may not always agree with me, but he is always there to cheer me on.

A Heckuva Family Vacation

As I mentioned before, we had the pleasure of taking our whole family along for the ride to Hawaii. But, of course, that didn't come without its own share of trials—particularly with four kids under six: a six-month-old, two-year-old, four-year-old, and six-year-old. We got separated at the Los Angeles airport with only a one-hour connection. Brooke's mom, who was with two of our four kids and a slower walker, hitched a ride on a motorized cart but somehow went to the wrong gate. We made the flight though. Once in Hawaii, we piled into our rental van, and my oldest, Olivia, started screaming when we discovered thousands of ants crawling under her floormat—an apparent problem in our fiftieth state. Thanks to jet lag, during our week there, the kids were dead tired by 6:00 p.m. and wide awake come 3:00 a.m. Though I was worn out before the race started, we made it work and truly had a life-changing experience. I wouldn't want it any other way.

Kona during the IRONMAN World Championship is surreal, it's impossible to describe. You have to experience it to understand. Although you plan to just go and relax and take it all in, it's overwhelming. It feels like you're at the Olympics. You're surrounded by all of these amazing athletes. You see 70-year-olds who look 50—not an ounce of fat anywhere on their bodies; everyone is parading through town in their speedos or spandex. Even in restaurants. No one is in normal clothing—it's all triathlon gear. The town is completely taken over with racers, and it is completely euphoric.

Dialing It Down

At Kona, I had what I considered a great race, despite the diarrhea I mentioned in the flash-forward at the start of the book. The overall result (my finish time of 10 hours, 45 minutes, 49 seconds), the feeling of truly giving it my all, and the knowledge I couldn't have done anything differently—it was all too good to be true. That's why I decided to go out on top, to quit aiming for a sub 10-hour Kona finish—I had already crossed it with pride and no regrets. I decided that while I could continue to compete at some level, I no longer needed the gratification of competing in the full IRONMAN distance. I had other goals to knock down.

I also didn't want to jeopardize my marriage, because there's no way I could keep training 20 to 25 hours a week, raise our four (soon to be five) kids, and be the kind of dad and husband I wanted to be. Brooke made huge sacrifices to support my dream, and I often ask myself, could I have done the same?

I shared with Brooke my plans of "slowing down" on our flight back from Kona. Although not fully believing me, she agreed—knowing I'd always be trying to one-up myself otherwise.

I will do another full IRONMAN some time when the kids are older. What's hard for me is I can't just do an IRONMAN just to finish. If I do one, I want to race it competitively and give it everything I have. Sometimes I envy those who race just to finish, but deep down I know that's not me. I'd rather not race, or do any competitive event for that matter, if I'm not trying to be competitive. It's hard for many people to understand; it's just how I'm wired and that's how I approach everything in life. I'm an all or none kind of guy, but maybe that will change as my kids get old enough to do stuff with me. No way I'm going to let them beat me, but it will be awesome to share the experience with them. When they finally beat me, they will know they earned it.

As of this writing (2018), I have limited myself to just four weekends of racing, competing only at the IRONMAN 70.3 distance. I've been fortunate to qualify for IRONMAN 70.3 World Championships the past five years, taking us to amazing places like Mont Tremblant, Canada; Zell am See, Austria; Mooloolaba, Australia; and Port Elizabeth, South Africa. In 2017, Worlds was in Chattanooga, Tennessee—so I competed in Edinburgh, Scotland to get in an international excursion for the entire family. The timing of Worlds is always within a few days of our anniversary, making qualifying an extra bonus—we normally stay the week after the race to celebrate.

I can't stay away from opportunities to compete, especially ones that allow me to continue to do what I love without compromising what's most important: my family.

Feeding the Addiction

I have several goals, one being to qualify for IRONMAN 70.3 World Championships every year. The hardest part of attaining a certain level of fitness is you want to continually test your limits. What's next? What else can I do? You know physically and mentally there's not much you can't do. It basically comes down to what are you willing to give up to pursue those goals. That's the thing; it's not that you have to do it to prove it to yourself, but you feel *compelled* to do it. I often struggle with being given this unbelievable gift and fear the potential regret of not maximizing it when the day comes to call it quits. I know my days are numbered, but I can honestly say if it ends tomorrow I have no regrets. As my kids continue to age, I am constantly balancing being active and engaged in their sporting events while maintaining my fitness. I could be faster if I committed the time others do, but that would require missing my kids' events which is something I'm not willing to sacrifice. It's a tradeoff and one I'm happy to make. My race selection is based on their "open weekends" but with five now in sports, three on year-round travel teams, its getting nearly impossible.

I aim each year to earn the IRONMAN All-World Athlete (AWA) Gold ranking, a designation for the top 1 percent of IRONMAN 70.3 racers. I've managed to accomplish this the last three years out of the four since the AWA ranking launched. As of the time of writing this book, I've completed a total of 25 IRONMAN 70.3 distance races and four full IRONMAN distance races, including competing in seven IRONMAN/IRONMAN 70.3 World Championship events. I've been extremely blessed to race in seven countries on four continents with Brooke at my side.

I have to keep reigning myself in so as not to overextend myself—that's how people get in trouble. So many lose sight of what's really important in life until it's too late. I have relished the results I've achieved in IRONMAN racing, while staying engaged as a husband and father. I truly believe God is using me to tell His story and has rewarded my faith in Him. There's a lesson to learn in every race, especially when everything goes wrong. I take great pride in having finished all 62 races I've done so far and never quitting, regardless of the challenge. There is a time and place for everything, and I take solace knowing I could be faster, but being an active father and husband means more than any podium finish. I love my wife and kids and thank God every day for blessing me with such an amazing life.

No matter your circumstances, if you can articulate your dreams and show you're doing the hard work to make them happen, others will likely step up and do what they can to help. Everyone wants to be a part of a winning team. My life is a living testament. I never could have gotten to where I am on my own. Sharing your dream with the world allows others to live out their dreams vicariously through you. And if you are lucky enough to have a family as supportive of your endeavors as I have, then you're already golden.

EAR DIARIES PART VIII:
CHECK YOUR POCKETS

When I first got my prosthetic ear, it took a lot of getting used to. Keep in mind I went 26 years without a right ear. I have to take it off when going to bed, take it off when exercising and take it off when I take a shower. One particular day following bootcamp class, I quickly showered at LA Fitness and rushed out of the gym to navigate the 45-minute commute to the office.

I was at the office sitting in a meeting when all of a sudden I get a text from my friend Mike Miller, that says, "Hey buddy, did you forget something?" I feel in my pocket and ascertain that I have my car keys, cell phone, wallet. I respond, "No, why do you ask?" He then tells me I left my ear in the locker room, but he left it at the front desk for me. So I called the front desk and asked, "Did anyone turn in an ear?" Complete silence on the other end. I said, "Yes, you heard me correctly. I have a prosthetic ear, and I accidentally left it on the bench in the dressing room." The manager excitedly replied, "Hey wait a minute, I have something all wrapped up here. Let me look inside this wad of paper towels." He goes "Yeah, I think this is yours." It was. I stopped by the gym on the way home.

IRONMAN
Wisconsin 70.3

Madison, Wisconsin

Life doesn't always go as planned, and IRONMAN races for sure don't.

Three months before IRONMAN Wisconsin, I was having left shoulder pains and learned they were because I had a torn rotator cuff, a torn labrum, and tendinitis in my biceps. I was a hot mess. Lifting my shoulder was a chore in itself, and under guidance from my doctor, I didn't do any swimming leading up to the race and resolved to just power through the pain on the swim—its only 1.2 miles. Race-day morning, there was a torrential downpour complete with lighting. The race director delayed the race thirty minutes to let the storm pass, but not before huge droves of racers turned in their timing chips, because conditions were absolutely horrible.

Transition was a complete mud fest. We and all our equipment got drenched setting up in transition. I conceded my swim would be miserable having not swum in six months. My goal was to just get out of the water alive but still thought maybe a top 10 was possible with a strong bike and run. I logged an all-time low—49 minutes—but honesty, I was happy, as I was essentially only swimming with one arm. I'm so glad the rain created the chop to give me an extra challenge.

I felt great on the bike until I got two flat tires before mile 11, leaving me stranded on the side of the road. I decided to once again run barefoot for a mile pushing my bike when I finally reached race staff who was able to call the mobile tech van; I stood there for almost an hour freezing, shivering from the cold. The Trek mobile techs said they were repairing flats all day—the roads had chip-tar sections with loose debris that had penetrated my tire and tube. I pounded on the pedals to not make my time a complete embarrassment, and I probably pushed a little too hard. I could have easily just coasted on the bike and run since I was out of contention, but I wanted the satisfaction of knowing I gave it everything, and I truly suffered. What's the point of training so hard if you're going to just call it quits because things don't go as planned? I race like I live my life … to the fullest, even when no one's watching and there's nothing to be gained (other than knowing I gave it my all).

I finished up with a respectable run and successfully completed what I set out to do, finish the race—although it was my worst finish (6 hours and 8 minutes)—and not hurt myself. All in all, I was happy that my record of consecutive races without dropping out remained intact. Sometimes races like this give me a lot of satisfaction, as I know I'll never quit even though everything says otherwise. Life tempts us to take the easy way out but we have to stay true to the cause and finish the task at hand.

CHAPTER 9

A Faith Unmatched

In order to mold his children, God
has to melt them down.
—Unknown

Kona 2012 was great, but life didn't stop there. I had more to accomplish, as a father, an athlete, and a businessman. Were it not for my success in business, I wouldn't have the means to do the things I do with my family, like take my wife to Austria and Australia or the kids to Scotland and Yellowstone. I strongly believe you have to get out and see the world to truly appreciate all your blessings. Life is all about experiences, not what you see on TV. You have to get out of your comfort zone and say "yes" to new experiences. I jokingly tell Brooke we may be broke and living in a shed in a few years, but we're going to have a blast in the mean time.

Also, unlike TV, life is not glamorous and without hardship. Even as the blessings continue to roll in, life is always going to throw you a curve ball. One of our family's most recent experiences with hardship was one that threatened the life of our youngest child, little Stella.

Faith Through Fire

There is nothing I have wanted more in life than to have a wife and kids of my own. Death is natural, and we all know it will take us one day or another, but we assume it will take us before our children. As a parent, there is nothing more sacred in our life than our kids. There is nothing we wouldn't do to prevent the suffering of our kids, but we also realize we can't take away all the bad things in this world. Instead, we have to rely on our faith to guide us through these moments of despair to help us embrace these soul-searching times for the stronger individuals we and our children will become. June 10, 2016, watching our two-year-old Stella fight for her life, was one of those days.

It is often said *you never truly appreciate life until you are about to lose it.*

Our sweet little Stella suffered a complex febrile seizure lasting more than two hours and had aspirated, destroying her lungs. She was rushed to Monroe Carell Jr. Children's Hospital at Nashville's Vanderbilt University, where she was put on a ventilator in an induced coma. I will never forget the image of my sweet baby lying there lifeless on our floor with EMTs working frantically to stabilize her, convinced she was brain dead. The next 10 days were a roller coaster of emotions. She desatted several times, experienced narcotic with-drawal, and formed a blood clot in her leg. The measured responses of the doctors let us know they were equally concerned.

The pain of watching her lying in the bed, the ventilator breathing for her, bandages enshrouding her head, and her body wrapped in a sea of tubes became unbearable. I finally had to get out of the PICU and clear my head, have a moment to reflect on the gravity of the situation. I decided to take a jog through the Vanderbilt campus. With every step I felt the weight of Stella's struggle being lifted. I asked God for strength, strength to trust in Him and to restore her to my arms. As I prayed aloud my pace quickened. With every stride I felt I was breathing for Stella; I was pumping life back into her. My pace was effortless; I felt a new sense of purpose and renewal. Four miles later I was back at the hospital and at ease, comforted. The weight of the world had been lifted. I knew then and there she'd be OK.

> **Sometimes it takes a serious wake-up call to remind us all of what truly matters.**

We're extremely blessed—and it's a miracle in itself—that Brooke was sitting beside Stella when it happened and didn't panic; my wife is always amazing in intensely stressful situations. I was also extremely thankful I was almost home from a crazy travel schedule and able to be there with her. Two years have now passed as of the writing of this book, and little Stella is as feisty as ever. And my faith is stronger than ever; it grows stronger and makes me stronger every day. Sometimes it takes a serious wake-up call to remind us all of what truly matters.

Bury the Obstacles

Success has never come easy for me and has always been disguised as a major obstacle. People see the lifestyle my family and I have now but have no clue as to the difficult decisions and sacrifices we have made thus far—with Brooke and I always on the same page. These include losing our house to foreclosure, applying for financial aid for the kids' school, and having to move in with Brooke's mom with four kids for three years to save money. We were struggling on one income to make ends meet. Those three years in my mother-in-law's house in Franklin, Tennessee provided an incredible learning experience and forced me to grow. Times were tough, but we didn't quit, and we didn't blame everyone else for our circumstances. I took responsibility for my decisions and knew that only the man in the mirror was to blame. Like my IRONMAN training, I finally mapped out how I would provide the lifestyle I wanted for my family and committed to making it happen: no excuses.

> **Success has never come easy for me and has always been disguised as a major obstacle.**

It was there in downtown Franklin that I rented an office where my officemate coincidentally turned out to be my old fraternity brother, Travis Anderson. He would end up introducing me to many important people, including his dad—the county mayor. Travis and I had coffee every morning, talking about how to grow business and network. That connection allowed me to leverage my insurance background into health care, doing workers' compensation billing and collections for hospitals. Surrounded by talented colleagues, I turned around my history of being the 1 percenter with bad luck—

remember, if there's a 1 percent chance of something going wrong for me, it will—to become a man in the top 1 percent of sales producers. I never could have guessed, from all those nights I stocked shelves in the hardware aisles of Home Depot for $12 an hour, that one day I'd be sharing my journey and offering advice with those looking to jump-start their own careers.

But as I've done throughout my life—after the fire, through IRONMAN—I had to work hard to meet my goals and take the road less traveled. In my six years as senior vice president of client services, I exceeded even my greatest expectations. It was a great opportunity, I enjoyed the people I worked with, and the timing was right. I felt like it was something I was meant to do. As soon as I took the job, I was asked to be a keynote speaker at the Georgia Health-care Financial Management Association (HFMA) conference, and that was the start of my motivational speaking. My boss encouraged me to share what he saw as a phenomenal story. He saw it as a message that would be welcomed in the health care industry and one everyone could relate to, because we all face obstacles.

Speaking to Adversity

Being able to share my journey from getting burned to becoming a competitive IRONMAN with people all over the country has been a blessing. At some point, we all have faced insurmountable odds and felt the

My message focuses on teaching people obstacles are opportunities in disguise. Our greatest disappointments in life are preparing us for our greatest blessings.

road ahead was just too hard. We've all contemplated, "Why bother?" My message focuses on teaching people obstacles are opportunities in disguise. Our greatest disappointments in life are preparing us for our greatest blessings—we just have to be willing to keep the faith and continue doing what we know will make us successful, even if we're not seeing immediate results.

Speaking at health care conferences and hospital leadership retreats is especially rewarding. I truly believe what I tell them: "I am one of your best success stories. The challenge is you see people like me at our worst. You never see us, and the lives we go on to lead, 30 years later."

In retrospect, I believe there are three things that have helped me become successful in overcoming my obstacles. These things have certainly gotten me to where I am in my career, but they were only possible with faith in God and the belief that success doesn't happen overnight.

First, I trained my brain. My entire life I have been fascinated with people overcoming insurmountable odds, whether it was Earnest Shackleton's endurance exploration or Colonel Sanders peddling his chicken technique. The more I read these epic stories and the conquest of the will to live, the more I realized they all had a common trait: a relentless and fervent pursuit of a better life. Over time, I have trained my brain to recognize opportunities amongst the daily distractions of everyday life (like meeting a stranger at Starbucks who would write me a check for $10,000). Once I started to identify what those things or situations are in life that contribute to success, my brain focuses on those elements as opposed to all the negative things in life. I have reprogrammed my brain to believe that

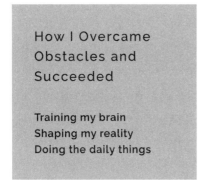

How I Overcame Obstacles and Succeeded

Training my brain
Shaping my reality
Doing the daily things

when, not if, I encounter a life or death situation, I will survive. My first reaction will not be *I'm going to die.* It will be *I'm going to thrive!* My brain will automatically start processing survival techniques and focus on a solution. By training your brain, you can block out all the distractions in life that deter you from achieving your goals. Don't let the minutia of day-to-day struggles be a distraction from doing the work necessary to obtain your goals.

Second, I shaped my reality. Don't subscribe to the victim mentality. Life is not fair and bad things happen to good people. Once you accept it, life is pretty simple. When something bad happens, know someone has been through something worse and not only survived, but thrived. Part of shaping my reality was learning to laugh at myself and not take life so seriously. The world can be cruel, but you don't have to let it defeat you. Don't hide from your insecurities. Use them to your advantage—it makes you distinctive and memorable. Confident people can be self deprecating because they don't need your approval to have a high sense of their worth. I realized early in life my self perception influenced how others perceived me. When my actions and mannerisms conveyed I was a fragile burn kid (i.e. Freddy Krueger), that's how others treated me. When I started acting like a champion, I exuded confidence and eventually my behavior became a self-fulfilling behavior (i.e. All-American triathlete). When we feel we are unworthy or undeserving of success or love, subconsciously we engage in behavior to limit our achievement and growth. You have the power to shape how others see you. Show them what a powerful, confident, and self-assured person looks like.

Third, I did the daily things. One of the things I ask at conferences is: "How many in the room could do an IRONMAN—a 2.4-mile swim, 112-mile bike ride, and 26.2-mile marathon?" No one raises a hand. I say, "Okay. Well, if we met tomorrow morning, how many of you could do a run-walk for fifteen minutes. We're not judging on speed. How many of you could run-walk for fifteen minutes?" All hands go up. I say, "OK, so what if we meet the day after that? How many of you could ride a bike for thirty minutes? Again, we're not judging on speed. How many of you could physically ride a bike for thirty minutes?" Of course, everyone raises their hands. Then I say, "Well, guess what? In thirty weeks of doing the daily things and building with each day, you'll be ready for an IRONMAN. Every one of you told me you couldn't do it, but when I walked you through what you need to do each and every day, you said you could do that." Doing the daily things also means doing the hard work even when everything says not to. Many nights after a long day of travel, I'll go to my pain cave and hammer out a 40-mile bike ride or a 15-mile run at 10:00 p.m. Could I skip the workout and my fitness not suffer? Maybe. But I do the workout because I know 99 percent of people would skip it. Do what others are unwilling to do and success will come. On the same note, there are times when you just can't get everything done. It happens and you can't beat yourself up over it. Tomorrow is a new day. Start fresh and resolve to not make it a habit.

There are so many things in life we never attempt because we can't figure out how to get started and what we need to do each day. But if you just start, and you have a plan, you can do it.

People always have excuses as to why they can't do something. Trust me, if you really want it, you'll figure out a way.

You're too old? Remember Madonna Buder from earlier in the book? She is the Iron Nun. At 82 years old, she became the oldest IRONMAN finisher. Of course she tells everyone, "I have an advantage. I have God on my side." She didn't start competing until she was 55 and is still racing triathlons at 88. Sister Buder believes

"Don't pay attention to how old you are; only focus on how old you feel."

You have bad knees? Let me introduce you to Rajesh Durbal. Raj is a triple amputee who not only completed Kona, but finished in 14 hours and 19 minutes. After completing the swim with just one arm, they had to physically carry him out of the water and set him down next to his bike so he could attach his legs to start the bike portion. He normally beats 10 percent of the competitors in the race. Forgive me if I fail to have sympathy for your aching knees. The beauty of IRONMAN is they hold everyone to the same 17-hour cutoff standard, regardless of your situation. When they say "*Shay Eskew, you are an IRONMAN*," you can truly brag the rest of your life because you know you did what 99 percent of the world would never attempt.

My Grass is Greener

I believe you can never rest on your laurels. No one cares what you did in high school, in college—or even last year. Top achievers only care about what they can do tomorrow, next week, and next year. It doesn't mean we don't take satisfaction in what we've achieved, but rather we believe we must continually innovate and evolve to remain on top. It's hard for people to understand how I can walk away from something when I'm having success. For me, it's always about being challenged and working toward a higher goal. Once

> In business, much like the game of life, perseverance and grit will be rewarded.

I've mastered something, I long for the next challenge and discovering what's possible. Success just happens to be a byproduct of enjoying what you do and committing to excellence. In business, much like the game of life, perseverance and grit will be rewarded.

Last year I walked away from the highest paying job I'd ever had, not because I hated it, but because I wanted a new challenge. I wanted the challenge of building an unparalleled sales team and change how health care sales were done. I wanted to evolve from being an independent contributor and building my brand to building a championship team and creating a company envied by all.

When news spread, people were shocked I could walk away from a very lucrative position. I'd be lying if I said it wasn't hard, especially with five small kids at home. Money obviously helps, but I'm more driven by the chase, competing and building something bigger than life. I know if I commit everything I have to being successful in whatever role I take; the money will come. I spent the last 17 years consuming every sales and business book I could get my hands on, as well as personally contacting extremely successful sales leaders. One such solicitation had a profound impact on my life. I emailed Jack Daly via LinkedIn with a snippet of my story and asked if I could buy him dinner in exchange for words of wisdom. If you don't know Jack, I highly suggest you do. He's an extremely successful, no nonsense man who exudes passion. Jack also is a Kona IRONMAN and has ran 95 marathons across all seven continents. After meeting Jack, I knew we were cut from the same cloth.

Thirty minutes into our conversation, Jack asked why I reached out. I told him, "My CEO asked me to contact you in hopes you'd talk me out of doing what I've already done: quit my sales job to pursue a sales-leadership role." Needless to say, two hours later he said, "I get it. You did what I did. You mastered what you were doing and now you're ready for the next challenge." In parting, Jack said I needed to write my book and he sent an introductory email to his publisher, Advantage Media Group. I signed with them a week later. One thing I learned early in life is to always listen to successful people. *Rule #1: When someone successful invests in you, do what they say!*

I am a consummate experimenter with sales strategies and buyer behavior and have risked substantial personal wealth to test my beliefs. I've reached a point in life where I want to teach others how to be successful, how to master adversity and create overlooked opportunities. I want to build a legacy. I had to make a hard career decision, but it was the right decision. I never looked back. *Rule #2: Never look back. Never!*

Thank God Brooke has always supported me and knows I would never put our family at risk. If you know me, I don't make rash decisions without extensive due diligence. I also wanted to be able to tell my kids I didn't stay in a job just because of money. I wanted to tell my kids I passionately pursued my goals and I was willing to do whatever it took to be successful. *Rule #3, Be the person you want your kids to be proud of. Be passionate.*

Other 1 Percenters

No one finishes the race on his or her own. We've all had a helping hand; Lord knows I have. If it weren't for the Shriners, I don't know where I'd be today. As such, I feel compelled to help others deal with their struggles in hopes I can provide hope. One thing I know is we all face obstacles, whether it be physical, mental, or spiritual. Over the years, I have spoken with numerous burn survivors and their families about the long road to recovery, even sitting with them in the hospital burn unit. One story in particular hit close to home: Alfred Real, also eight, lived in Atlanta, treated by the Shriners, and also set afire by a neighbor's kid.

On June 12, 2010, I received a Facebook message from my longtime friend Jennifer Hatfield. "A friend of a friend's eight-year-old son was badly burned last week. He's in Cincinnati and stable at this point, but he has a long haul ahead of him. When I heard the news, I was immediately taken back to the day that I heard about your accident." Two months later I was able to meet with Alfred. I shared my burn photos from 1982 and how my scars progressed over the interceding 35 years. I also showed him pictures of me wrestling and progressing to IRONMAN as well as compared stories of the compression suit and orthotic braces (he was outfitted in the same gear). Finally, I assured him time is a great healer. Since then, it's been amazing to watch him recover and get on with his life.

One of my greatest joys is speaking to school kids of all ages. I have spoken to my kids' elementary classes and without fail I'm asked to take my ear off for everyone to see. The poor teachers are always caught off guard, but I know they're equally curious. I can only imagine the discussions at dinner tables: "Mom, Maddox's dad took off his ear today."

I'm also the annual speaker at the Rotary Youth Leadership Awards (RYLA) program—they love me taking my ear off too. I love sharing my struggles in coming to terms with my deformities as a teenager, definitely my hardest years. I'll never forgot one particular shy ninth grader in 2012. I told the group "When you look like me, you have to own it, or it will kill you!" This young lady broke down as she ran from the room. I received a call from RYLA Director Bob Huffman stating how within 24 hours of my presentation, she was a changed person. A week later a thank you note arrived addressed to Bob. The young girl wrote about my talk and the impact my story had on her life by writing "His talk literally saved my life." She had underscored "saved my life." Kids need to learn it's okay to be different and not be perfect. We're perfect in God's eyes. The world is far from perfect and when they're adults, they'll learn that standing out in the crowd can truly be an asset.

Besides sharing my story, I also participate in multiple service projects through the IRONMAN Foundation. We do service projects in the communities we race in order to "demonstrate service through sport and commitment to community." Local projects have thus far included teaching at-risk kids how to swim, restoring a watershed, packing supplies at a Food Bank, and raising over $50,000,000 in funds.

The Eskew family collectively participates yearly in a Christmas-basket program our church does in partnership with GraceWorks Ministries. In our community, it's easy to think everyone has plenty, especially as you sit in the pick-up lines at school and see a parade of Mercedes, BMWs, and Land Rovers. But there's another part of our community that is out of sight and the struggle is very real. With the Christmas-basket program, my kids are able to hand-deliver groceries, toys, and bikes to families in need and see the joy on their faces when receiving things we take for granted. The gratitude these families express is priceless, and I pray a little of it rubs off on my kids.

Like Peanut Butter and Jelly

God rewarded my faith in him by providing an amazing wife who loves me unconditionally, Lord knows I test her patience. I know everyone thinks being married to an IRONMAN must be awesome, but it comes with a price. Jokingly, I always remind Brooke neither of us will do well in a singles bar with five kids, so we have no choice but to ride this train: we're damaged goods. I'm sure every wife has stories about "you won't believe what my husband did," but here are a few of hers:

- On our honeymoon, I dismissed her suggestion that we'd need the tops to the rental jeep for the three-hour, one-way trip on the "Road to Hana" in Maui. Needless to say, we encountered monsoon like rain and got drenched for two and a half hours of the drive.

- We had just bought a really nice bed for Olivia, and I strapped it to the roof of our SUV for the four-hour drive from Nashville to Atlanta. Brooke felt it was not strapped correctly, but I assured her "No problem, babe. I got this." Naturally, the bed flew off the roof of the SUV at 70 miles per hour on Interstate 24.

- Every year I light up our house at Christmas with about 10,000 lights, always tripping breakers when it rains. As we were leaving town for the weekend one year, Brooke suggested we unplug the lights. "What? It's not going to rain" I told her. We came home three days later to complete darkness. Fear overtook me as I realized the deep freezer storing six months of her breast milk was without power.

- I bought a huge bookcase complete with a rolling ladder for our house. Brooke suggested I go home and remeasure, since the bookcase was non-returnable. "Of course I measured and, yes, it fits, trust me," were my last words. We soon discovered the bookcase was too tall to fit through our doors and had to pay a carpenter to cut it in half and then reattach it. She was very proud of me.

- The day before our summer family trip, this time to Boulder, Colorado, I was going through emails, wondering why I had not received a message from Southwest to check-in. I then noticed I had booked our seven flights for July instead of June. The last-minute flight increase was triple the original cost. I had already prepaid our Airbnb and car rental. We also had just bought new hiking boots for the kids, mapped out the entire trip, and there were no other dates for the entire summer we could take vacation. With no other alternative, I bit the bullet and paid the triple airfare but decided to keep my little mistake to myself to preserve the vacation experience. Brooke is finding this all out for the first time in this book.

Our marriage has survived 15 years of chaos (as of 2018) and produced five amazingly energetic and fun-loving kids. It hasn't always been easy, but I couldn't imagine it any other way. Every time the chaos seems unbearable, I remind myself of parents with chronically ill kids or those who wanted kids but could never have them and how they would give anything to experience our chaos. It's all about perspective. Like my IRONMAN racing, it took years of hard work and lots of give and take. For starters, we knew what we wanted. We had a plan and we never deviated, even when the cards were stacked against us. We wanted four kids, all to be about two years apart and were going to wait two years to have kids after getting married. We also agreed it was best for the kids for Brooke to stay at home full time once the first child was born. True to form, we had *five* kids (obviously lost count) and all exactly two years apart (with February,

March, April, May, and June birthdays). With every kid came additional challenges, but somehow, we've always adapted.

My wife loves me dearly, but she is not a fan of my motivational or inspirational messages when applied to her. One of my favorite things to do when I occasionally wake her when getting up at 4:00 a.m. is to whisper, "Hey, Babe, are you going to make a difference today?" I'm always careful to be out of striking distance when doing so. The normal response is "SHUT UP! Leave me alone." I will then call her later in the day and say, "Hey, Love, have you done it? Did you make a difference yet?" She usually just hangs up. We go together like peanut butter and jelly.

FIND WHAT DRIVES YOU

When I first moved my little family to Franklin, just 20 miles south of Nashville, my income dropped 35 percent, and we had no option but to live with Brooke's mom. Trust me, it was the last thing I wanted to do, but I knew God was humbling me and he did a great job. We didn't panic; we stayed the course. It was hard, especially on my ego. No man wants to admit he's struggling to provide for his family and needs help. Brooke offered to go back to work but we both knew we needed her at home with the kids. The stress at times was unbearable and everyone was quick to offer unsolicited advice.

Every person faces a "make it or break it" moment but not everyone realizes those circumstances when they happen. For me, it occurred after a networking event with my fellow Lambda Chi brothers at a local pub. On the way to my vehicle, one of my fraternity brothers made an offhanded comment, "Hey man, everything ok? Things must be pretty rough if you're living with your mother-in-law and driving that SUV." It was a 10-year-old SUV and he remembered the BMW I had driven prior to getting married. I shrugged it off and commented "Actually, things aren't so bad. The SUV is paid off; we're saving up some money to buy a house and kids are healthy. Luckily it's all temporary and things are about to change."

His comment was exactly what I needed although I didn't want to hear it. I knew then and there I had to fight like hell and do everything I could to make it happen and make it happen now. This was my chance to prove I had what it took to be successful and nothing was going to deter me. The unsettling circumstance forced me to make a big career change and fearlessly pursue success as if my life depended on it. To me it did, as well as to the lives of five others. Fear is often our best motivator. I feared letting Brooke down, letting my kids down, my parents and all who knew me. I knew I was capable of so much more. When our backs are against the wall, that is when we experience our greatest growth. Pain is a great motivator. When the pain becomes bad enough, eventually we will do whatever it takes to make the pain go away—or give up.

For me, giving up has never been an option. You have to look within and find what drives you.

Just six years later, my income increased tenfold, but not by accident. I became more intentional with everything I did with the end in mind. I was laser focused to only commit to activities that could contribute to achieving my goal of providing a better quality of life for my family. If there was no correlation to my goal, I said "no." I said *no* to watching football games with friends. I said *no* to weekend bike rides with large groups. I said *no* to grabbing a beer with the guys. It wasn't because I didn't want to; it was because I knew it wouldn't help me achieve my goal. Saying *no* to goal distractions is the most empowering feeling. When you're questioning whether something is a good use of your time, just ask yourself *"will this help me achieve my goals?"* If the answer is *no*, put your head down and move on. And if the answer is *yes*, commit 110 percent to make it work and don't let anyone deter you. Many have tried to deter me from reaching my goals, but I have held firm because I knew I had a higher calling and an obligation to my family. If you can't do something amazing for yourself, do it for those you care about. Let them be *your why*.

Like my IRONMAN training, I knew I needed specific goals and benchmarks for measuring my progress. I had just read *The One Thing* and came to the conclusion "the one thing" I could do to impact my career was to get in front of people. I've always believed if I was just afforded an opportunity to meet someone, I could create a memorable impression. If I created a memorable impression, they're more likely to help me achieve my goal whether through directly buying my services or indirectly through introductions to other influential people. My goal was to meet as many people as possible in the business community and establish credibility. I knew the investment of time to create a network, combined with a commitment to help those in my network achieve their goals, would pay huge dividends down the road.

I put a plan in place to increase my network and relentlessly met with as many people as I could. I joined the local Rotary club. I became active in our church. I volunteered for as many community events as my schedule would allow. I had standing coffee meetings with respected peers just to brainstorm on how to grow business. I sought out successful entrepreneurs to get insight into their success. I devoured every leadership and sales management book I came across. I not only read them, but I took notes and applied their principles.

During that era in Nashville, I found that it was my family driving me to succeed. But I have always been stabilized by my faith: faith in myself, faith in family, and faith in God.

· · · · ·

I still turn to the same three places for strength, faithful that these three things will get me through: myself, my family, and God. Faith is what has seen me through countless fires. Pushing myself to the limits, filling my lungs with air, and clearing my head brings me to a special place; it's a place I've turned to ever since I first began to see what the fire could ignite. It's a place where I can count on finding that inner strength and sense of self I have continuously discovered in every baseball game as a kid, every wrestling match in high school, every boxing match or near-death experience I faced in college, and every race I've competed in since. The place I go to in these moments has shaped me and will always be a place of solace, where I know I can return to who I really am and remember where I've been. It's there that I can clearly see how life's worst helped me achieve my best.

EAR DIARIES PART IX:
MR. POTATO HEAD

It was 2012, and I was at the New Jersey Healthcare Financial Management Association Conference in Atlantic City. It was well attended, with about 400 people at the event, but the conference was a first for me. That evening, there was a big social event, complete with live music and a dance floor. During an impromptu dance off, they formed a big circle out in the middle of the dance floor, and people took turns in the middle, doing their 10 to 15 seconds of showcasing their moves.

And if there's one thing about me, it's that I love dancing. Going back to my high school days of taking country dancing lessons to pick up girls, dancing has always been a great source of enjoyment for me.

So, I boogied out in the middle and worked the floor, throwing everything into it, bringing the house down, and I finished it off with a back-spin breakdance move. When I stopped, I jumped in the air, threw my hands up and there's complete silence. I'm like, "Are you kidding me?" I saw the competition—no way anyone else was even close. I was a little upset, but then a friend of mine says, "Shay, your ear is still on the dance floor."

No one else knew me, so they didn't know what to think or how to react. I casually strolled back, grabbed it, and popped it back on. There were certainly whispers, and I don't really know what they were saying. But I'm sure was something like, "Wait a minute, did we just see that?"

CONCLUSION
Zero Regrets

The pain that you are willing to endure is
measured by how bad you want it.
—David Goggins, Navy Seal

The most powerful lesson I've learned, in sports and in life, is that you are so much stronger than you may ever know. Sadly, so many in life seek to avoid pain at all costs, failing to realize the embracing of pain can lead to self-actualization. Growth comes at a cost, but it's one we're all capable of paying. Perseverance can overcome the lack of athleticism or natural abilities. So many people look at me and assume it's natural talent that's helped me excel in IRONMAN and business. On more than one occasion, some have said, "You're so lucky. Things just come easy for you." They assume they don't have the talent, so they quit, not realizing a lot of the great ones are great not because they're naturals, but because they worked hard at it. They spent years persevering and sacrificing. It's all about how badly you want it.

I learned as a kid that life is not fair, but it's too short to make excuses for not being successful. Although I didn't have the easiest childhood or one I'd wish for any of my kids, I am thankful God has worked miracles with my mom and helped her find a happy place. Words can't express how grateful I am for having a father who showed me what unconditional love is, and how you love those you care about even when they are incapable of loving you back. My story is also a testament to how a couple committed to each other can move mountains.

I've always figured, if I can survive everything I did as a kid, I can survive anything I'll face as an adult.

One of the biggest questions I'm always asked is, if you could go back to that day, August 4, 1982, would you do anything different? Would you still walk across the street and tell Becky about the yellow jacket's nest? If you'd asked me that question when I was 10, 18 or even 25 years old when I was still trying to come to terms with everything, I would absolutely say "heck no." Who would intentionally want to endure everything that I've had to go through?

But now that I'm on the other side of things, and I've seen all the blessings I've received as a result of what I've endured, I absolutely would do it again. There is nothing I would do differently ... except maybe burn off my left ear too so they'd match and I'd be more balanced.

> **"**
> Getting burned
> is quite possibly
> the best thing to
> happen to me.

I've made lots of mistakes, but I have no regrets. Getting burned is quite possibly the best thing to happen to me. Name just one thing in life I've ever missed out on as a result of getting burned. I'm a husband to a beautiful woman. I'm a father to five amazing kids. I have an immensely successful career that I love, that I've built from the bottom up. I'm a motivational speaker with the opportunity to have an impact on countless strangers. I'm a world-ranked IRONMAN competitor, and I've never not finished a race: 62 races as of this writing and going strong. Did I have to work five times as hard as everybody else just to be average? Absolutely, but because I had to work five times as hard, everything meant 10 times as much to me. I take a lot of pride in the small things because I know what it's taken just to get me to this point. That's why, before every surgery, you'll find me in my hospital room exercising. I know if I wake up and I can't run or I can't walk, that I can accept it because I made the most of every minute. If you were to look at life that way, I believe your own life would take on a different meaning.

Getting burned gave me gratitude, mental toughness, tenacity, grit, and competitive drive. It gave me a sense of humor. It gave me charisma, too, and a little of that can go a long way.

> **Anything you've gone through, someone else has gone through it and survived.**

We all have a story, and I would never compare what I've been through to anything that's happened to you. We all experience pain differently. However, I can assure you, anything you've gone through, someone else has gone through it and survived. It's all about embracing the hand you've been dealt and running—in my case, quite literally—with it.

If you're comfortable with your shortcomings, others will be too. Embrace them. Don't hide them. Learn to make fun of yourself, and to take life less seriously when you can. Share your story with others, and talk about your struggles. We all face adversity in one form or another—physical, mental, or spiritual. Sharing creates bonds that help us better connect with those around us.

Good things always result from pushing forward when everything else in life says quit. It may take longer than you'd like—it took me decades, actually, to realize what the fire ignited—but I hope my story gives you encouragement to carry on through the dark times. You will get through it, and when you do, *you really do* have the strength to rise above it. Then you can begin to see how life's worst can help you achieve your best.

IGNITE YOUR FIRE

1. Make a difference today.
2. Quit talking about it, just do it.
3. Commit to doing the hard work. Always.
4. When you compete, compete to win.
5. Never lose because you weren't prepared.
6. Give 110 percent in everything you do.
7. Be memorable. Stand out.
8. Remember what's really important.
9. Spend time with successful people.
10. Laugh at yourself daily.
11. Embrace the suck.
12. Live as if tomorrow is no guarantee.

ACKNOWLEDGEMENTS

N o one leads an empowering and successful life without help. I believe God puts people in our lives who can have a profound impact on our future if only we get out of our comfort zone and take the first step. Initiating simple conversations with complete strangers has resulted in someone at Starbucks writing me a check for $10,000, someone convincing me to write this book, and a Grammy-award-winning singer asking her fans to vote for me to race in the IRONMAN World Championships. These chance encounters, I prefer to call them divine interventions, impacted my life. I truly believe if you are passionately pursuing your dreams, others want to help. I've been fortunate to have so many supporters over the years, many advocating on my behalf without my knowledge. I am fearful of trying to highlight all acts of generosity for fear of excluding so many, but some have went the extra mile.

It's amazing how many lives have been impacted by the Shriners. Every time I share my story and their role in my healing, someone always says "They treated me too." The Shriners truly were a life saver. We were barely making ends meet with no way to pay the two-million-dollar hospital bill. They afforded us compassionate care givers and provided the best care for over 13 years at no cost. I often wonder what would have happened had the Shriners not got involved.

In 2012, Joel Shapiro had the most expensive cup of coffee in Starbucks history, but he helped a complete stranger (me) achieve his lifelong dream of competing at the IRONMAN World Championships. I'm grateful beyond measure for Joel's generosity and his introduction to his business partner, Todd Ehrlich, who played a major part in the effort. Their combined support allowed my family to cheer me on at the finish line in Kona and to celebrate one of my greatest accomplishments. Achieving a life dream is awesome, but having those you care about the most there to celebrate with you is beyond comprehension.

I don't know why Jack Daly answered my LinkedIn email on November 18, 2017: "I'm reaching out to see if I could fly out and share a cup of coffee, morning run, bike ride, etc. and gain some insight ..." Two months later, Jack and I met. At the end of our dinner he asked "When are you writing your book?" Long story short, Jack said "Quit making excuses and write the book. I'm going to introduce you to my publisher when I get back to the hotel and the rest is up to you." I don't know what I did or said to convince Jack to help, but I can never repay him for the push I so desperately needed.

In January of 2000, I responded to an internship posting in our MBA career office. Once I interviewed and learned I'd be working on a daily basis with Mike Crabtree, I was sold. Mike imparted his financial expertise, life lessons, and cautionary tales as all great mentors do. When I was contemplating a career change in 2017, Mike was able to dissect months of my soul-searching and within 30 minutes helped me formulate a vision for my path going forward. I can't thank Mike enough for his ability to bring clarity and focus and isolate all distractions.

ACKNOWLEDGEMENTS

Words can't begin to express the gratitude of a newbie, who was just breaking into the sport, having a well-respected shoe company like Newton Running take an interest in my story and treat me like a professional. Wendy Lee made me an informal Newton Ambassador after receiving my email in 2011—they were still very much a small startup company. I have been running in Newtons ever since and loving every mile of it.

I could never thank my wife Brooke enough for her unconditional love, friendship, and support of my neurotic tendencies. Who would have thought this persistent, pushy, one-eared burn guy with scars covering over 65 percent of his body would find a beautiful wife willing to overlook everything on the outside and see me for who I am? She is my best friend and soul mate and has always been by my side, for the best of times and for the worst of times. Loving me can't be easy, but together I know we can overcome any obstacle thrown our way.

Nothing in life prepared me for the joy of having five kids. Whenever life's challenges seem overwhelming, I remind myself how lucky I am and that I will never quit because these five little ones are counting on me. Olivia, I love your competitive drive and desire to be the best. Never lose your hunger to compete and remember believing in yourself is contagious. Maddox, I love your inquisitive mind and quest to always find the true meaning of things. You have the ability to unlock many of life's mysteries. Asher, I love your kind heart and desire to truly make people feel better. You are a soothing soul and I know you have so much hidden talent waiting to be unleashed. Beckett, I love your happy-go-lucky attitude and ability to hang with the big boys and mix it up. You are always smiling, and those big blue eyes and mischievous grin light up a room. And Stella, I love your princess warrior attitude and spunk. God almost took you from us, but I know He has big plans for you and for that we're eternally grateful. I pray you show the world what your mother and I see every day. You all gave me a renewed purpose in life and I will never forget my pledge to be the best dad I can be.

Thank you, mom and dad, for always being there and supporting my journey to do the impossible and never giving up on me. The road hasn't always been easy, but we made it. You always believed God was watching over me and never lost faith in Him. Thank you for making all the sacrifices over the years to help me be the best version of me.

Although I'm 13 years older and she was dragged around to many of my wrestling matches as a toddler, my sister Britney has been a great supporter and was there when I crossed the finish line of my first IRONMAN. We even raced together at the Rock 'N Rollman series in Macon, GA—I did the half while she did the sprint. It has been rewarding watching her grow into a loving mother and wife. I am so proud of her.

Thank you to my grandparents, Rachel and Harold, for being my home away from home as a child and always making me feel loved. I'm also extremely grateful for my Aunt Gail who has always treated me as one of her own. Thank you to my Uncle Steve for always entertaining me and being one of my biggest fans. I'll never forget the times we had together when I was a kid.

Special thank you to my mother-in-law Marilyn (Nona) who helped us any time we were in a jam and never said no. Nona has been a great spiritual leader for us and made sure we never slacked in our obligations to our faith. Thank you to my father-in-law Bill Etherton who watches down from heaven. I am so thankful you gave me your daughter's hand on September 6, 2003 and entrusted me with one of your most beloved possessions. I wish you were here to experience your grandkids and this crazy journey we call life. Also, a special thank you to Joe Cat, Yogi, Aunt Vin, and Uncle Mike for cheering me on at my first triathlon, my first IRONMAN, and spearheading the team Eskew cheer club from afar at countless other races.

Words cannot express the gratitude I have for the impact Henry Forrest had on my life. In such a short time, through his actions and his words, he showed me what it was like to be a man's man. A man loyal to his country, loyal to his wife, and loyal to his Heavenly Father. Even as he was dying, he showed all of us how to live courageously. Were it not for his battle with pancreatic cancer, I would not have found my destiny in IRONMAN. Semper Fi, Henry!

My desire to truly define what was physically possible introduced me to some of the most amazing athletes in the world, world champions actually. Over the past 10 years, I have learned that what makes Craig Alexander and Chrissie Wellington so amazing is their humility and their generosity with their time. They are great ambassadors for the sport and actively impart their wisdom to others.

Behind every great athlete is a great coach. I am thankful for the introduction to Adam Zucco of Superfly Coaching. Adam elevated my game to new levels, helping me qualify for IRONMAN 70.3 World Championships for four consecutive years. Thank you, Adam, for your attention to detail and investment in your athletes.

I wonder what kind of man I would have been had it not been for wrestling. I am extremely appreciative for Coach Rollie Lambert taking me under his wing as a sixth grader and teaching me how to compete on the mat. Coach Keith Gossett provided the support and teaching I needed as a freshman to prepare me for varsity wrestling. I don't know how life would have turned out without the influence of Coach Gordon Pritz. He taught all the wrestlers how to train, how to push beyond the pain, how to battle until the whistle blew, and how to never quit even when all appeared hopeless. Most of all, he made all of us men. Coach believed in us and we never wanted to disappoint him. We learned so many life lessons in the wrestling room that made us better husbands, fathers, and men of God. As he preached to us, pain is temporary, but pride is forever.

I had the best team at Advantage. Thank you to Kelly Smith, Eland Mann, Lauren Franceschini, Melanie Cloth, Saara Khalil, Keith Kopcsak, and the countless others behind the scenes who helped me pull this feat off. Without your help, there was no way I could finish this book in record time.

If God doesn't work in mysterious ways, how do you explain the introduction of Brigette Hyacinth (a bestselling author from Trinidad) into my life? We were both keynote speakers for a healthcare conference and I had been following her LinkedIn posts for the past year. Unsolicited, she endorsed my book and attracted over 500,000 views on LinkedIn and hundreds of book orders. Thank you, Brigette, for your genuine sincerity, desire to help others, and commitment to excellence.

Lastly, thank you Lord for all of my blessings. My life is evidence grace exists. You have given me my strength and you have never abandoned me in my times of need. Regardless of the challenges ahead, I always knew you were lifting me up and would never give me more than I could handle. I am eternally grateful for my life journey and wouldn't trade my experiences for the world. Through my pain, you have shown me love. Your love knows no boundaries. Please help me ignite the fire of others so they can embrace obstacles as opportunities in disguise.

ABOUT THE AUTHOR

As a childhood burn survivor who became an IRONMAN World Championship competitor, Shay Eskew became an author because he has lived a life that is stranger than fiction. In addition to enduring 35-plus surgeries, losing an ear, and having scars cover 65 percent of his body, Shay has also competed in nearly 70 triathlons thus far, including 10 World Championships, in unbelievable conditions across four continents.

A one-time bear research biologist and bear attack survivor, Shay is a motivational keynote speaker for conferences and leadership retreats around the globe. Before his career in health care, Shay did it all—from driving a dump truck to selling hardware at Home Depot.

Shay has been a Newton Running Ambassador and an IRONMAN Foundation Ambassador since 2011. He is also an inaugural cohort of the IRONMAN Foundation Mālama Club, an exceptional group of passionate triathletes who are committed to creating positive, tangible change in race communities. He currently resides in Brentwood, Tennessee with his five beautiful kids, his very patient wife, his German Shepard, and, of course, one serious home gym.

Follow Shay's blog or book him for a speaking engagement by visiting shayeskew.com.

OUR SERVICES

Shay Eskew inspires audiences around the world with his motivational message of never letting life's obstacles deter you from achieving your dreams. He went from learning how to walk again to racing across seven IRONMAN World Championship finish lines on four continents. He lives his message and has helped countless others achieve their dreams. His goal is to help individuals and organizations quit making excuses and make a difference in their life. Learn how to live a life of purpose and to embrace the journey of transforming obstacles into opportunities.

Want to make a difference? Want to live a life where anything is possible? Want to be the person you've always dreamed of being? Take the first step. Commit to doing whatever it takes and never quit!

Character development areas:

- Turning Obstacles into Opportunities
- Goal Setting and Measuring Results
- Reclaiming Time, Savoring Every Minute
- Leveraging Adversity to Build Character
- Building Grit and Mental Focus

CONNECT WITH SHAY!

Website: www.shayeskew.com

LinkedIn: https://www.linkedin.com/in/shayeskew/

Twitter: @ShayEskew

Instagram: @MrShaySQ

FaceBook: https://www.facebook.com/ShaySQ/

Email: shay@shayeskew.com